How We Work

How We Work

Live Your Purpose,

Reclaim Your Sanity, and

Embrace the Daily Grind

LEAH WEISS, PhD

HARPER WAVE

An Imprint of HarperCollins*Publishers*

HarperCollins books may be purchased for educational, business, or sales promotional use. For information, please email the Special Markets Department at SPsales@harpercollins.com.

FIRST EDITION

Library of Congress Cataloging-in-Publication Data has been applied for.

ISBN 978-0-06-256506-8

18 19 20 21 22   LSC   10 9 8 7 6 5 4 3 2 1

This book is dedicated to anyone who has had the Sunday blues.
A new Monday has finally come.

Love and compassion are necessities, not luxuries. Without them, humanity cannot survive.

—DALAI LAMA

Contents

How We Work

Introduction

A shoe repairman spent long, tedious days fixing people's shoes. He worked seemingly endless hours to make a modest living, and over the years, he grew frustrated by the unrelenting monotony of his work and the struggle to make ends meet. His job felt like a dead end, but he lacked the resources and social connections to find his way into a more fulfilling or lucrative career. Eventually, he met a teacher who made some simple yet profound suggestions as to how he could bring a different quality of attention to his work fixing shoes. Figuring he had nothing to lose, the shoe repairman practiced these new skills every day, paying attention to his tasks differently, and in time, his experience of work was completely transformed. His job didn't change, but he did.

This man lived a little over a thousand years ago, as the parable goes, but his story has endured, and his predicament is relevant to many of us today. Partly because work is where we spend so much of our time and partly because of its nature, nothing provides more opportunities than the workplace for us to feel discouraged, disappointed, bored, overwhelmed, envious, embarrassed, anxious, irritated, outraged, and afraid to say what we really feel. Like it or not, aware of it or not, we feel things at our jobs, and how we feel at and about work matters—to us, to our families and friends who are impacted, to the quality of our work, and ultimately to the success of the organizations we work for.

This is the bad news that at some level we already know too well: work hurts.

A recent report from Gallup, the largest database of workplace research, offers evidence that the old workplace ways (annual reviews, forced rankings, outdated competencies) no longer achieve the intended results. The American workforce has more than one hundred million full-time employees. One-third of those employees are what Gallup calls "engaged at work." They love their jobs and they make their organizations, and America, better every day. Conversely, 16 percent of employees are found to be "actively disengaged"—that is, they are miserable in the workplace and destroy what the most engaged employees build. The remaining 51 percent of employees are "not engaged"— they're just there. These figures, I believe, indicate an American workplace philosophy that simply doesn't work anymore. One wonders if the country's declining productivity numbers point to a need for major workplace disruption. Indeed, one of the top recommendations of the Gallup report is for organizations to "Change from a culture of 'paycheck' to a culture of 'purpose.'"

Another study, the 2016 State of Enterprise Work Report, showed that 76 percent of workers interviewed said the main reason they work is to pay the bills. Yet at the same time, 92 percent felt it was important for their work to be rewarding.

What many people don't realize is that these two goals—a paycheck and a sense of purpose—need not be mutually exclusive. And yet many of us are "not engaged" or worse—truly suffering. The paradox is that being mindful of our experience of our work, even to our dissatisfaction, disengagement, and ambivalence, is the first step toward turning it around. Indeed, paying attention to our feelings is the very definition of mindfulness.

Contemplative traditions such as Buddhism have long recognized the value of mindfulness. More recently, scientists have found methods to observe and quantify its benefits. For more than a decade, I've been teaching mindfulness as a method for personal and professional growth, most recently at Stanford's Graduate School of Business, where I teach a course called Leading with Mindfulness and Compassion. That title may sound like what one of my students suggested when he asked, "Is this going to be a bunch of hippie BS?" Yet being mindful is a critical skill for young aspiring leaders, and among the personal attributes that fall under the category "soft skills," a term coined in 1972 to capture the social and interpersonal capacities that are the foundation of our ability to effectively work with others. Hiring managers say that the most vital of these skills include communication, adaptability, creativity, and demeanor.

In 2015, the *Wall Street Journal*[1] conducted a survey of nearly nine hundred executives. Ninety-two percent of those surveyed said that soft skills were just as important as or more important than technical skills. And here's the kicker: 89 percent of those surveyed said they were having trouble finding employees who possessed soft skills. Similarly, a survey of 291 hiring managers by LinkedIn found that 59 percent said they had trouble finding job applicants with exceptional soft skills, and 58 percent said that this fact limited their companies' productivity.[2]

The millennia-tested, evidence-based strategies I share with my students, and that I will share with you, allow us to view the work we do as an opportunity to practice mindfulness, purposefulness, and compassion. I offer these strategies not merely as coping skills or as a means of reducing stress and getting through another day at the office, but because they can *enhance* your experience of the workplace and of life.

Much like the pterodactyl whistle that announced the end of Fred Flintstone's workday, today the old boundaries that delineate the professional and the personal (career and family, business and pleasure, even secular and sacred, as we will see) are neither realistic nor relevant to the way we work or would like to work. We all want our work to matter and want to matter to our work. Whether you're a corporate employee, a freelancer, a teacher, a health care provider, or a hedge fund manager, you probably want to care about your work beyond the time you're on the clock. While flexible hours are the most sought-after workplace benefit and can help engender more engagement, they also cause the boundaries between work and the rest of our lives to become more porous.

Given this reality, what can we do?

In the Tibetan language, *heart* and *mind* are expressed as the same word. Mindfulness practice, or *lojong*, is often translated as "mind training," but I prefer to use the term *heart-mind training*, which keeps the heart in mind. The *lojong* system was popularized by twelfth-century meditation master Chekawa Yeshe Dorje, who recognized that integrated practice (that is, one that allows a student to practice anywhere, doing anything) would be a good fit for working people. With this approach, the teacher meets the students where they are: brothels, battlefields, schools, businesses, monasteries, even bars. (This doesn't mean the teacher recommends that the student *stay* at the bar, but it's a starting place.) For example, you can start where you are now. Mindfulness belongs on the train ride to work, in an office cubicle, behind a cash register. In fact, modern neuroscience and behavioral science research suggests that mindfulness training belongs anywhere and everywhere we spend our time.

This book is about how we work. When we pay attention to the thoughts and feelings we have about what we do, they can be our greatest resource for courage, creativity, meaning, and resilience. When most people hear the term *mindfulness*, they think of meditation, the sitting-quietly-doing-nothing version of meditation—which is obviously not appropriate workplace behavior unless you're on a break. Yet this thinking is too narrow—and too bad. In fact, the Tibetan word *gom* that is customarily translated as "meditation" can be more literally rendered as "familiarization." Forget incense and the lotus position, forget notions of "getting rid of thoughts" or "navel gazing," meditation is, more broadly and more helpfully for most people, getting to know our minds and hearts. When it is done right, it allows us to get to know the places where our mind "goes" and, over time, to get better at putting it (gently) where we want it to be. We come to know what our heart really wants, and we improve our ability to listen to it. By this definition, we can practice meditation anytime, anywhere, on the spot. Work becomes an opportunity for us to train ourselves to have more conscious and compassionate intentions and to hold ourselves accountable to those intentions in the kindest possible way. When we make these choices regularly enough, these new behaviors become familiar to us. In a word, they become habits. As such, not only is meditation compatible with work, but we can also think of work *as* meditation, wherein each moment of the workday is an opportunity to train our hearts and minds in good habits.

I like the phrase "work as meditation" because it has this paradigm shift built into it: it doesn't make any sense by the narrow definition of meditation as sitting and doing nothing. On the whole, I use the term *mindfulness training* more than *meditation*. In my experience teaching thousands of people from all backgrounds and in many different contexts, the term *meditation* comes with too much baggage, and all that weight makes it seem like a drag. (I once caught a typo in something I'd written: where I'd meant to type "mindfulness," I'd spelled it "m-i-n-d-f-u-n-l-e-s-s." Perhaps this was my subconscious telling me to lighten up, but the error did seem apt: meditation and mindfulness often get bum raps as merely two more heavy, burdensome items on the long list of "should-dos" we beat ourselves up for not doing.)

So, while meditation has come to mean one thing to most people (sitting meditation), mindfulness training is quite flexible, and general enough to include all kinds of approaches to working with the mind, gut, and heart, from formal sitting practices and retreats to thought experiments. All of these methods allow us to find the existing interstitial moments and places in our lives where we might catch our breath—what the Tibetan tradition calls "natural meditation." Natural meditation is not closing your eyes and working at it. Rather, it involves accessing a mental state that is familiar and always available (a state we often miss because we are in such mental overdrive), setting your intention, and engaging in perspective-shifting "micro moments"—all of which you can do at any time of day.

To be clear: I'm not *against* sitting meditation. I teach it and I do it—not as often or for as long as I did when I was in my twenties, when I spent a hundred days each year on silent retreats, but I have a practice that works for me now. Still, sitting practice doesn't need another advocate; there are other, lesser-known and often misunderstood routes to mindfulness that do.

In mindfulness training, there is no separation between what is meaningful and what is mundane. We can practice with anything. The back-to-back demands and busyness of our days do not stand in the way of our purpose in the world; they represent a chance to realize it. With mindfulness, we take our challenges as opportunities and our adversaries as teachers. We practice seeing the best in others and we do the same for ourselves—not naïvely, but intentionally and strategically. When we look at it this way, we're freed from what I call the scarcity mind-set: that constant, nagging feeling that there's never enough time or resources and that we're not up to the task of living our life. In this way, nothing and everything changes.

The single most important takeaway from traditional mindfulness training is that it teaches people to see their thoughts and feelings as *just* thoughts and feelings rather than as something loaded with meaning that defines who they are. It is the difference between being *in* the fray but not *of* it. This is a big deal, with tremendous practical implications for our day-to-day lives. Recognizing that you feel afraid of change, but remembering your purpose and intention, can give you the courage to take a new job or relocate somewhere unexpected. Noticing the urge to lash out at a coworker, yet remembering to have compassion for who that person is and where he or she might be coming from, can result in more allies and fewer regrets. Mindfulness training means learning to do things differently. In Buddhist tradition and modern psychology alike, mental action *is* action, as consequential as physical action.

When I first got the Buddhist meditation bug as a fifteen-year-old, I was motivated by existential questions about meaning. I wanted to understand why there was such inequity in the world, what could be done to change racial, financial, and gender disparities. I was frustrated that the people around me didn't seem to care about these matters, while they were all *I* could think about. In high school, I took a class called Literature of Enlightenment with a teacher who was a longtime practitioner of meditation. There, I came upon Tibetan Buddhism for the first time—and felt as if I'd found a long-lost friend: the ideas made more sense to me than anything I had encountered, and I identified strongly with them. Still, I didn't yet practice diligently. When I finally got my butt on the cushion in a much more serious way, in my twenties, meditation became a tool to cope with the suffering I was experiencing—my father was diagnosed with the cancer that eventually took his life and a close childhood friend passed away in quick succession. For the next decade, I spent my time participating in, variously, one-hundred-day and six-month-long meditation retreats, all while pursuing degrees first in social work and then in pastoral counseling, and then getting a doctorate in education and theology. While I was working on my dissertation, I reached out to the Dalai Lama's interpreter Thupten Jinpa, to interview him about my topic: adapting Tibetan compassion practices to meet the needs of trauma survivors. Partway through our conversation, he asked me what was behind my interest in the topic, and I told him of the work I was doing with health care providers looking to treat the problems associated with burnout. He invited me to join an invitational retreat weekend at Stanford that would be attended by a hand-selected team of scholars and teachers, and the next thing I knew, I had been asked to become the inaugural director of education at Stanford's Center for Compassion and Altruism Research and Education (CCARE).

It was at this time that I connected with Pat Christen, CEO of HopeLab, for her insights on how best to set up and run the Compassion Center's teacher training program. A research and development nonprofit that seeks to motivate behavior change through the design of video games, HopeLab was born of philanthropist Pam Omidyar's hunch that gaming could serve the interests of children with cancer. Later, HopeLab expanded its focus to look at resilience more broadly—and the research was showing that the kind of work I did with compassion and mindfulness was what led to increased resilience. I soon fell in love with the culture, content, and team at HopeLab, and after having two more babies, I spent a few years working full time there, in collaboration with the Compassion Center but focusing the majority of my time on research, writing, and developing my own program for Stanford's Graduate School of Business (GSB) and for work with veterans.

When I set out to write this book, each iteration of my initial proposal forced me to leave my comfort zone a little bit more. I asked myself a question from the ten-thousand-foot view: How can the ancient principles that have so impacted my life help people solve the problems that most impact their lives?

For the majority of people who practice mindfulness, simply being mindful is not its own goal. It is a path toward something else.

Research at HopeLab pointed to the instrumental role that strong purpose, social connection, and agency play in increasing resilience. When I learned this, I had a flash of insight: that purpose was the ultimate goal and that the practices I'd learned (mindfulness, self-compassion, and compassion) helped one realize one's purpose.

Over the course of the five years I've been working on this book, my life has evolved along with it. I went from being a full-time working mom to my one-year-old daughter to a full-time working mom to three children ages five and under, with growing professional demands on my time. Our family lives in the San Francisco Bay area, one of the most expensive places on earth, and neither my husband nor I have chosen financially lucrative career paths. There's not a lot of physical space in our home, and chaos rules most days (and nights). As a working mom, I find that much of my time is spent trying to prevent the plates I've got twirling around in the sky from crashing down on my head. And I know from the parents I hang out with at pickups and drop-offs and in parks all over the peninsula that we are all swimming in this soup of scarcity. So, with each new school semester, I've tried to develop more and more streamlined approaches to mindfulness practice. Rather than beating myself up for not meditating two hours each morning, I've tried to adopt the viewpoint that HopeLab espouses: that it is not helpful to put together an optimal intervention that no one in the real world can use. What *is* helpful is to create the minimally viable version of an intervention that will have an impact.

This revelation became the koan (or paradox) that has informed how I think about my practice, my teaching, and this book. My guiding question became: What is the smallest thing a person can do to move the needle on the pain he or she is experiencing? The best way to figure that out wasn't through a lot of thinking and talking; it was through generating a plausible idea, creating a prototype, testing it in the real world with real people, and reflecting on what had been learned.

Suddenly, I saw things framed differently: I actually had plenty of time to practice, I realized, because practice wasn't something I had to take time out of working or mothering or living to do. In fact, working, mothering, and living—life—were *all* opportunities for practice. There is a saying in the Mahayana tradition of Buddhism: "Take all of life onto the path." Freed from the confines of the cushion, meditation could include all of life.

We in the West have been missing the point of meditation. It has never been about sitting quietly with our eyes closed. Those of us with a meditation practice can too easily forget that the point is not to become better meditators, while those without a practice rightly wonder what the point *is*. The very traditions that brought us meditation include a metaphor for this confusion: Sitting meditation is a boat we can take to a destination. This boat is only one of many vehicles that can get us where we need to go. The person who gets too attached to meditation as an end in itself—to "being a meditator" and telling other people that they should meditate—is like a poor schmuck carrying a boat over his head instead of simply walking. Since the 1970s, when Buddhist leaders in exile from places such as Tibet came to America, and interested Westerners who trained in the East brought back Eastern teachings, there has been no shortage of books on meditation or teachers of meditation—to the point where many people think there are only two choices: carrying a boat over their heads or not getting to their destination. This book is about walking, so to speak, and is a reminder of the destination: not to escape this world but to be of greater benefit to ourselves and others in it.

In short, we can't wait until we feel we have enough time to practice mindfulness. As a mother of three young children, I can attest to the near impossibility of adding another project to my life. The list of things I'm already not doing for myself is a mile long. And I know I'm not the only one in this situation. Even with the structure and support of a class, most of my students, across the many different populations I teach, find it practically impossible to keep up a sitting meditation practice. Even at Google, where the most popular extracurricular course offered to employees is an eight-week meditation program called Search Inside Yourself, I've been asked by the human resources department to advise on off-the-cushion awareness and compassion practices that can be integrated with regular work, because most Google employees either don't take the course or feel they can't find time to practice meditation the way the course teaches it. As one Googler put it in our first meeting, "F*** classes." He loves classes, I love classes, but sometimes classes aren't enough. It's about what we do *outside* class that impacts our work experience and what we contribute to our organizations.

Working people need an integrated approach to mindfulness training. This is true for leaders as well as the people they lead. They have stuff to get done; they need to keep working. We all do, even if we aren't CEOs, because we are all leaders of our own lives, in our families, and in our communities. We need a practice where we don't have to do something different so much as look differently at what we're already doing.

I like to think of this notion of practice as "applying the wax." In many sports, athletes apply wax to their gear to decrease resistance and improve performance. You can ski cross-country and hit every patch of resistance, or you can apply wax to your skis and make the same path feel effortless. Mindfulness, then, like that wax, becomes something we use that allows for optimal performance. We need to "apply the wax" while we're driving, when we get ourselves a cup of coffee, when we talk to a colleague—in short, in all we do. This takes almost zero extra time, as little as a few seconds—what Marc Brackett at the Yale Center for Emotional Intelligence calls a "micro moment," which is enough time to reset our perspective. This is a different, equally valid, more complete, and, for the vast majority of working people, more realistic approach to mindfulness and meditation (and

to interpretation of the texts and teachings of Buddhism) than the traditional adaptations we commonly see in the West.

On our first day of class, I tell my students, "We're going to learn
how to change our relationship with our existing habits of thinking
at and about work, and find freedom in the new possibilities that will
emerge as a result." By the end of our time together, my students (most
of them, anyway) say that the course profoundly changed the way they
understood leadership—of companies perhaps, of people probably,
and certainly of their own lives. I know objectively (from pre- and
post-mindfulness practice measurements) that my students' feelings
of loneliness, their mindfulness, and their thriving all move in the
right direction. According to them, the course helps them "sleep at
night," "find" themselves, and get ready for "the real world."

Prototype, experimentation, and informed redesign—the contemporary Western system for innovation known as "design thinking" that
is de rigueur all over Silicon Valley—has a surprising analog in a two-
thousand-year-old Tibetan system called *dampa sum*. Literally, and
rather poetically, *dampa sum* means "good in the beginning, good in
the middle, and good in the end." This three-part mindfulness training instruction applies to everything we do or want to do. Not coin-
cidentally, I think, both design thinking and *dampa sum* trace the
basic structure of another famous learning strategy: the hypothesis,
experimentation, and conclusion of the scientific method. As a student, practitioner, and teacher of Tibetan Buddhism, I was struck by
these similarities when I came to HopeLab, and I've been exploring
this Venn diagram ever since. And it was in the overlap among Tibetan
Buddhism, science, and design thinking that I found my business
school course, and the structure for this book.

"Good in the beginning" calls for setting an intention for how we're
going to do something according to the result we'd like to achieve.

"Good in the middle" entails doing the thing. In this doing, our actions are informed by the clarity we've obtained by setting our intention. Finally, "good in the end" means reflecting on how it went (or how it's going, if it's still going on). In short, purpose (good in the beginning), practice (good in the middle), and reflection (good in the end). This goes for anything—a day, a presentation, a conversation, a moment—and it is a continuous feedback loop. Reflection informs our purpose going forward.

When you begin to apply *dampa sum* to everything you do, you will see its effects everywhere you look. For instance, in setting out to clean up your office, first you consider what you are about to do, what change you want to see. You intentionally connect it to your larger goal—say, of living a meaningful, productive work life. But knowing that alone does nothing; you have to actually clean your office. This is the practice part. Then, at the end, you have a result, which, in addition to a more hospitable work space, might include finding that lost document you thought you'd never see again. At this point, you might ask yourself (reflection) if the action you took furthered your larger goal of living a more meaningful and productive work life. And from there, you might set a new goal: whether to keep your office organized or simply to notice what gets in your way when you fall short on this. Ultimately, reflecting on the result of an action is how you learn that the trouble of doing that action was worth it, for example, or that you might want to do it differently next time. And no matter how ordinary the task may be, the long-term effects of the process can be profound. *Dampa sum* is about nothing less (and nothing more) than seeing clearly, putting your mind and heart into what you're doing, and understanding how you can change your experience by changing your perspective and behavior.

In Silicon Valley parlance, we say "fail" and "fail better." The fundamental idea, in twenty-first-century business as in twelfth-century Tibet, is that products and processes should be deeply informed by the experience of the people who employ them. For this to happen optimally, the user's insights must be integrated at every step of the way, from initial design (purpose), through testing the prototype (practice), to the "final" design, usually with multiple cycles of redesign to get there (reflection informing new intention). Of course, for so many of the products we use these days, the very notion of a "final" design is quaint. Every week, if not every day, some app or another on one of our devices needs an update. We might say we live in an age of iteration. After all, design thinking informs operations at elementary schools as well as tech companies. Yet Buddhists two thousand years ago recognized that we are always in an iterative age: good in the beginning, good in the middle, good in the end (and then start again from the new beginning). Thus, the overlapping, threefold logic of *dampa sum*, design thinking, and the scientific method becomes more than structure. As we will see, *dampa sum* is also a way of being in the world.

"Good in the beginning, good in the middle, good in the end" doesn't mean that everything always unfolds according to plan. It doesn't mean we always get what we want. It doesn't mean that bad things don't happen, that we don't get sick or old, that we don't lose people we love. It also doesn't mean that we all have to work for a Good Cause. It means we find the good causes all around us, the small opportunities for purposefulness, mindfulness, and compassion in everything we do, and this will manifest in our work and our lives in very real, tangible ways—sometimes big ways.

When people find out I teach mindfulness, they often ask me if their time on the elliptical machine—or commuting, or doing the dishes, and so on—"counts." My answer, based on thousands of years of tradition and reams of scientific evidence, is yes . . . *if we make it count.* Yes, even standing in line at Starbucks counts, if we take the opportunity to feel our feet on the floor, our impatience in the form of tightness in our shoulders, and if we have compassion for ourselves and the other people in line. In the same way, work counts if we make it count.

In the spirit of recognizing and acknowledging our common humanity (a fundamental of compassion training), this book unabashedly assumes that we are all in this together. And the data suggests a collective mind-set is more than just wishful thinking. According to Gallup, "Employees who are supervised by highly engaged managers are 59 percent more likely to be engaged than those supervised by actively disengaged managers." Like it or not, we are impacted by the level of engagement around us.

What would our work and our workplaces look like if we acted as though our colleagues were just like us? What if our bosses, our bosses' bosses, our peers, supervisees, people in our department, people in other departments, the guy with the goatee in HR, our customers, even (or especially) our competitors, and the service agents, store clerks, and other people whose work affects our lives every day—what if these human beings were all *just like us*? It's a serious question because they *are* just like us in important ways. It's a radical question because this is not the approach to work that won the day during the Industrial Revolution (obviously), nor is it one featured in most business books. Recognizing our common humanity means viewing workers as more than automatons. It means creating a truly humanized workplace, one in which people are seen, valued, engaged, and supported.

This book is for all of us who would like to have more influence over how we think, feel, and act, both at work and in our lives as a whole. I am sensitive to the very real impact that systems have on people, both positive and negative, and have therefore strived to make the strategies in the book realistic. I'm not naïvely claiming that we can solve all our problems with attitude adjustments. I'm not suggesting that a cleaning person has the same problems as a CEO. But I do believe that the principles and practices I share here, when grounded in experience, can change lives. Even in the specific environment of a business school classroom, my students are a surprisingly diverse bunch, coming from nonprofits and start-ups as well as multinational corporations and traditional financial institutions around the world. One student took my class between tours of active military duty. And in working with these people from diverse backgrounds, I've seen that, behind the particulars, their desires are the same: to matter, to belong, to do their best, and to pass that on. How we relate to our most human, tenderest vulnerabilities has a very real impact on our work and the people we work with, but work is the last place where we're supposed to acknowledge this. I wanted to challenge this taboo and write this book from my experience as a teacher, woman, and mother—for everybody.

Part I

———

HAVING PURPOSE AT **WORK**

It's Possible

1

Healing the Toxic Workplace

In the 1980s, architects began to design buildings with energy efficiency in mind. One of the ways they did this was to create structures with a "tighter envelope," or less ventilation. Around the same time, the first reports of "sick building syndrome" surfaced.[1]

Sick building syndrome was the term used to describe a cluster of symptoms experienced by people who spent their days in environments heavy in pollutants such as nitrogen dioxide, VOCs (volatile organic compounds), and allergens. Employers grew concerned about this mystery illness, as it was increasingly linked to diminished productivity and lost profits.[2] There was also widespread apprehension over the implications for the long-term health of people who worked in environments constructed with materials made of toxic chemicals. It was out of this concern that the "green" building movement grew.

In 2015, a team of researchers led by Joseph Allen at the Harvard T. H. Chan School of Public Health set out to collect data on the impact of sick building environments on the cognitive functioning of their occupants and to test the impact of various green building standards.[3] To do this, they set up a double-blind study—even the researchers didn't know which people were in which group—involving twenty-four Syracuse-area professionals. These architects, programmers, and creative marketing professionals went to work in simulated building conditions at the Total Indoor Environmental Quality Laboratory at the Syracuse Center of Excellence in Environmental and Energy Systems. They spent six full workdays (nine to five, with a forty-five-minute lunch break spent in a room adjacent to their work space) in offices that simulated conditions of green, green+ (better ventilated than the regular green condition), or conventional offices. At the end of each day, the study participants were administered tests designed to assess their cognitive functioning.

The researchers determined that cognitive scores were 61 percent higher in the simulated green building and 101 percent higher in the green+ environment than in the conventional buildings. All nine cognitive domains that were tested scored higher in the green or green+ buildings, with the biggest increases in functioning demonstrated in crisis response (97 percent higher in green and 131 percent higher in green+), strategy (183 percent higher and 288 percent higher), and information usage (172 percent higher and 299 percent higher).[4]

This study is regarded as a game changer for people in the construction industry as well as most forward-thinking, productivity-minded businesses that invest in healthy buildings for their employees. It offers evidence that the materials used to construct a building have a measurable impact on the people who work in that building. Indoor environmental quality is now a massive priority for businesses. Genentech, Kaiser, Google, Salesforce, Facebook—all are investing significant resources, to the tune of billions of dollars, in creating green work spaces. And in top-tier leadership training programs, such as those at the Harvard T. H. Chan School of Public Health and the Harvard Kennedy School, students are learning to include these considerations in their planning and decision-making processes.

Take the case of industrial engineer Ray Anderson. In 1973, he founded the company Interface to produce carpet tiles in America for institutional settings. The idea was to create new chemicals and materials following the common practices of the time—practices that paid little attention to the toxic impact these chemicals might have on the environment or the lives of the manufacturers and end users. Everyone was doing business this way. It was the accepted, dominant model.[5]

Twenty years later, while reading Paul Hawken's book *The Ecology of Commerce*, Anderson was struck by what then seemed a crazy suggestion: that business was the cause and also the only possible solution to the environmental catastrophe.[6] In fact, in *The Ecolgy of Commerce*, Hawken cites Ray Anderson (and Interface) by name as an example of unmitigated "plunderer[s]." In his 2009 TED Talk, Anderson spoke about the unexpected impact this had on his life. Rather than double down on his position as acting within the agreed-upon norms of his time, he heard this critique as a moment of sanity in an insane system—and as a call to action. He made the pledge to take from the earth only what could be renewed and to do no harm to the biosphere. "If Hawken is right, and business and industry must lead, who will lead business and industry?" he asked. As a self-described "recovering plunderer," Anderson saw the need to step up and lead his company to a new way of doing business. As a result, he created Networks, a joint effort between the Interface carpet company and the Zoological Society of London that repurposed old fishing nets into nylon carpets. This has created less toxic carpets and therefore less toxic physical work spaces, but it has also created a new paradigm for doing business.

I'm telling you this story because sick building syndrome is really about the toxic environments we work in, both literally and figuratively. Even if the buildings we work in go "green," what about the rest of the work environment? How do we make it better? Sometimes what is considered "normal" in a given time and place is actually insane. Mindfulness training gives us the wisdom to recognize when we are in a situation like this, and the strength to be the crazy person when needed.

Rehumanizing the Workplace

One of the greatest insights we've gained from the past fifty years of social psychology is that our environment matters. And while we are no longer subjected to the extreme working conditions of the kind seen in Upton Sinclair's *The Jungle*, we are dealing with a new set of subtler unsafe working conditions.

Americans work a lot. According to a 2016 survey conducted by National Public Radio, the Robert Wood Johnson Foundation, and the Harvard T. H. Chan School of Public Health, "almost two thirds of workers say they often or sometimes work overtime or on the weekend, and about one in five say [sic] they work 50 hours or more hours per week in their main job."[7]

The United States is one of the only highly developed nations in the world that does not guarantee workers some paid leave each year. And even when our employers do offer vacation days, many of us don't take them.[8] According to the same survey, less than half of workers who received paid vacation days used all or most of them in 2015. The survey also found that more than half of adults went to work when they were sick. In addition, 44 percent of respondents said their job negatively affected their overall health, and more than 40 percent said it negatively affected their family, weight, and sleep.

Most of us put in extra hours or skip vacations because we want or need to be more productive. But here's the thing: studies of both manual and white-collar workers show that once we put in forty-nine hours of work a week, our productivity not only levels off but begins to decrease. At a certain point, working excessive hours actually undermines our productivity. And with diminished time and energy to live our lives, this creates a sense of scarcity in our individual and collective mind-set.

In 2015, my friend and mentor Pat Christen and I presented at that year's Stanford Social Innovation Review Conference. Pat, who used to run HopeLab, is now the managing director of the Omidyar Group (of which HopeLab is a part), a collection of organizations and initiatives established by eBay founder Pierre Omidyar and his scientist-activist wife, Pam.

The research Pat presented at that conference was all about not having enough—enough time, enough money, enough sleep, enough exercise. She explained how existing in this scarcity mind-set day in and day out impacts our mental, physical, and emotional health and can lead to chronic problems such as addiction, obesity, divorce, depression, anxiety, loneliness, and burnout. She cited statistics showing that people who work more than fifty-five hours a week have a 33 percent greater likelihood of stroke and a 13 percent higher risk of heart disease. In addition, 35 percent of these workers reported that their jobs interfered with family time and were a significant source of stress.[9]

The data back up what many of us know to be true experientially: a lot of us are unhappy and unhealthy and outright overwhelmed by the demands of our jobs, and approaching the question of how to be okay or sane, let alone well and thriving, feels like another overwhelming idea. When the whole culture lives this way, it can be hard to locate where the problem lies or address the question of fixing it. The fact is we wear our busyness like a status symbol, and research shows that such aspiration holds real value—Americans who always say that they're "busy" are viewed as more important and of higher social status.[10]

We didn't plan to be stressed out or bored, anxious or overwhelmed, to feel like meaningless cogs in a very large wheel. Yet somehow too many of us do have this experience too much of the time. Nowhere more than at work do people struggle with the need to feel fulfilled. This need isn't limited to people who work in the obvious mission-driven fields such as education or in the nonprofit sector. It includes everybody—everybody who ever wanted to be something when they grew up; everybody who has ever felt they didn't know what they were doing and feared they would be found out; everybody who enjoys complaining about work more than doing it, who experiences the Sunday terrors, or who feels oppressed by information technology's tether, who doubts that a "work-life balance" is possible; every parent who finds herself between a rock and a hard place, struggling with ambivalence or full-blown guilt both for leaving home to go to work and for being distracted by work when at home; everybody who works too much and everybody who is trying to work more.

It wasn't always this way, of course. When we start a new job, we're usually excited about the opportunity and have good intentions to make the most of it: to support ourselves and our families, to learn something valuable, to move toward a goal. But this motivation doesn't necessarily trickle down to the stuff that makes up our days. We have to find something clean to wear and keep ourselves looking presentable, to be in several places at once and get to all of them on time, to keep track of our kids, to call our parents, to feed ourselves but not too much, to respond to texts and keep up with e-mails, hopefully to get some exercise, pay the bills, bake for the bake sale, get to the parent-teacher conference, and get our teeth cleaned. We have to worry about a lot of things: the health of someone we care about who's not doing well, a credit card balance that's not doing well, a child who's not doing well; what people think of us, how much they value us, whether we're getting the recognition and pay we deserve. We are, by turns, overwhelmed, ashamed, bored, angry, jealous—and we might simply prefer to be numb. It's no wonder we lose track of our original intentions.

Not only is all of this subjectively unpleasant, but also it makes us physically sick (that mind-body connection again), emotionally distraught, and mentally compromised. And it spills over into our lives outside work as well as the lives of the people we care about. What can we do, here in the real world—short of acting out our fantasy of screaming, "Take this job and shove it!"? Is enjoying our evenings and weekends and vacation days (if we are lucky enough to get some and not too busy to take them) the best we can do? Should we just suck it up? Is this what it means to be a grown-up?

In a word: no. There is a better way.

We live in a culture that values not only productivity but also profit and promotion at any cost, one that rewards jerks who elbow nice people out of the way, and that creates toxic work environments. Peter Frost, an early and influential thought leader on compassion in the workplace, once said of the office environment, "There is always pain in the room." This University of British Columbia business school professor who passed away in 2004 diagnosed workplace toxicity as a very real threat to employee performance and company goals. In his groundbreaking piece for the *Journal of Management Inquiry*, "Why Compassion Counts!,"[11] he points out that it is impossible to neatly categorize work as a rational place where emotions don't belong. In other words, there is no checking your feelings at the door. Yet this is what most of us attempt to do.

The bottom-line currency of the workplace is often used as justification for bad behavior. Stanford Business School scholar and tenured professor Jeffrey Pfeffer, who teaches a course called The Paths to Power and is regarded as one of the most influential organizational theorists of our time, wrote an article called "Why the Assholes Are Winning."[12] In it, he argues that there is a huge gap between the traits of good leadership (modesty, honesty, authenticity, and generosity) and the leadership styles of iconic CEOs such as Roger Ailes, Jeff Bezos, Bill Gates, and Steve Jobs, whom he characterizes as "ill-tempered and demanding" and exhibiting "abusive behavior with few to no adverse consequences."[13] But companies flourished under the leadership of these men, so their bad behavior was excused as a necessary cost of innovation and success.

Make no mistake: it is appropriate to feel sick in a sick environment. And in such an environment, we might well blame ourselves for our suffering, unaware of the role played by a toxic workplace. We are the frog in the pot of water that is slowly being brought to a boil: not seeing the flame or the pot.

The good news is that the curricula at the best business schools in the world are no longer just about learning to win at any cost. In these hallowed halls dedicated to teaching leaders how to make a lot of money, students are now also learning how to create better work environments and be more compassionate leaders. They're learning how to create new normals for the workplace: treating colleagues and employees with respect, communicating with candor, behaving with integrity.

In 2008, Harvard Business School celebrated its one-hundredth anniversary. That same year, the global financial crisis inspired a group of disillusioned HBS students to work with professors David A. Garvin, Rakesh Khurana, and Nitin Nohria to develop a "Hippocratic Oath for Managers".[14]

As a business leader, I recognize my role in society.

My purpose is to lead people and manage resources to create value that no single individual can create alone.

My decisions affect the well-being of individuals inside and outside my enterprise, today and tomorrow.

Therefore, I promise that:

I will manage my enterprise with loyalty and care, and will not advance my personal interests at the expense of my enterprise or society.

I will understand and uphold, in letter and
spirit, the laws and contracts governing my
conduct and that of my enterprise.

I will refrain from corruption, unfair competition,
or business practices harmful to society.

I will protect the human rights and dignity of all
people affected by my enterprise, and I will
oppose discrimination and exploitation.

I will protect the right of future generations to advance
their standard of living and enjoy a healthy planet.

I will report the performance and risks of my
enterprise accurately and honestly.

I will invest in developing myself and others, helping the
management profession continue to advance and create
sustainable and inclusive prosperity.

*In exercising my professional duties according to these
principles, I recognize that my behavior must set an
example of integrity, eliciting trust and esteem from those
I serve. I will remain accountable to my peers and to
society for my actions and for upholding these standards.*

This oath I make freely, and upon my honor.

The Hippocratic Oath for Managers received a great deal of media attention, and students at schools ranging from Harvard and the City University of New York to business schools in Japan and Spain have signed on. But the oath is not enforced by any external organization, and breaking it does not carry consequences; it's essentially enforced as an honor system. It's a great first step, but it does not attack a key area of concern: business education. If a student signs the pledge, he can try to self-regulate, but without comprehensive education that teaches him *how* to be successful and ethical at the same time, how can he make good on his oath?

When I interviewed Jonathan Levin, dean of the Stanford Graduate School of Business, I asked him how he felt about GSB's approach to education in values and ethics. He said that in addition to one required course early on that specifically addresses ethics, ethics are integrated into every course. The rationale is that when we are in ethically de-manding situations in the real world, there are no flags or whistles labeling them as such. This integrated approach to ethics is great in theory, but it is based on a voluntary effort from individual professors. There is no measure of how often ethics come up in discussion or how well students are prepared, and no assessment of or accountability for their ethical education (or their ethical behavior once they return to the workforce).

In the end, though, classes and pledges, while valuable, can take us only so far. As in life, ethics in business start at the level of individual action. Luckily there are things we can do to help us put ethics into practice on a daily basis.

Accomplish This: Create a Mission Statement

It is sometimes difficult to recognize when we are in a toxic environment, particularly when undesirable behavior is normalized or even practiced by management. The frog-in-the-pot metaphor works well here—in my first job out of grad school, I worked around the clock, was often stressed, lacked perspective, and ended up gaining fifty pounds. I didn't see the changes because they were so gradual. We naturally bring our feelings, opinions, and behaviors (some desirable, some not so) to work. In any situation, our strongest locus of control is our own performance and behavior. Knowing this can give us a lot of influence over our situations.

A mission statement articulates the core purpose and values of an organization. Writing your own mission statement, similar to an oath, can help you identify if you are living up to your ideals or falling short. You may not be the boss or the decider at work, but there are aspects of the situation you can influence. You can draft a personal statement that reads, "I will maintain my own integrity on the things that matter most to me, such as . . ."

If you are a business leader, you can create an oath that acknowledges your role in society by stating, "My personal leadership mission is to . . . and as a result, I commit to these actions and behaviors . . ." See an example of a personal mission statement here: www.leadhweissphd.com/personalmissionstatement.

Skills: Soft vs. Hard

Many industry leaders today complain about a shortage of "talent." They say that new members of the workforce lack the ability to handle the demands of our complex economy and socially complex organizations. The *Wall Street Journal* reported on a recent study by

DePaul University researchers that found that "managing workers and decision-making—two subjects that require softer skill sets such as being sensitive when delivering feedback—were most important to acting managers. However, those subjects were covered in only 13% and 10% of required classes, respectively, in a study of 373 business schools," said DePaul professor Erich Dierdorff, one of the study's researchers. "Part of the difficulty might be that soft-skill classes aren't respected as much as 'hard' courses, like finance, according to professors and students."[15]

Many business school graduates have mastery of the technical skills needed to land a job but seem to lack critical thinking skills. They may be able to program algorithms or fill out a spreadsheet, but they might not be able to write with ease, or communicate complicated ideas, or discuss difficult issues with colleagues. It's easy to scoff at the notion of studying self-knowledge and persuasive communication when quarterly reports are due and when your paycheck is tied to quarterly earnings. Indeed, some in the business world regard "soft skills" as, well, soft. Yet the truth is that students can't solve problems in a changing business landscape without these skills, many of which are formed and honed in a liberal arts context.

Soft skills are difficult to teach. They are also extremely difficult to measure, but we can measure what happens in their absence, and we can see how behavior is impacted when they are present. When the leadership research and training firm Leadership IQ tracked twenty thousand new hires over their first eighteen months on the job, they found that 46 percent of them did not last at their jobs or they underperformed in them. And, according to the U.S. Department of Labor, the price of a bad hire is at least 30 percent of the employee's first-year earnings. Of those failures, 89 percent were attributed to attitude; only 11 percent were attributed to lack of skill.[16] "Attitude" included such factors as motivation, temperament, low coachability, low emotional intelligence, and poor ability to receive feedback or collaborate.

This is where mindfulness comes in. Soft skills need not be framed as head versus heart (that is, being able to *either* think *or* feel). Mindfulness shows us that when we know what we are feeling, when we stay integrated as a whole person, our capacity to think, work, feel, and have positive interactions with others is improved. The fact is we need all ways of knowing at different times in our lives and work, and we need to know when to apply what. Without this ability to think critically, to have meta-awareness of our context and our methods for engagement, we cannot create plans for what should be done, and we certainly cannot lead others effectively to execute those plans. In short, we have to have wisdom as well as knowledge.

So how do we implement mindfulness at work? A good first step is to use meta-cognition, which means tapping into our purpose while we perform our daily tasks and tracking where we are putting our attention. Focusing on the conversation, task, or challenge at hand, without allowing our minds to wander, helps increase our sense of purpose and reduces stress. Consider how your daily work connects both to your personal goals and to those of the organization. How do the two intersect? Clarifying this in specific ways can be empowering. It can also help you map out a plan so you know which tasks to focus on for the day or the week. Next, check in with yourself to see how well you focused on the right priorities for optimal output. Finally, identify and eliminate distractions that take you away from accomplishing your goals. Are you spending too much time on e-mail? Helping co-workers on their own projects? Doing tasks you could easily delegate? By being conscious of distractions, you can more easily catch yourself falling prey to them and turn your focus elsewhere.

Mark Mancall, my longtime mentor since my undergrad days at Stanford, and founder of Stanford's famous structured liberal arts approach to interdisciplinary education, used to complain to me that the majority of his students were illiterate. He meant this in the sense not that they couldn't read, but that they couldn't meaningfully reflect on what they had read and then express it in their own words. Merely parroting information, for Mark, was akin to high-functioning illiteracy.

Business degrees buy jobs, which make business courses very popular. According to the U.S. Department of Education,[17] one in five bachelor's degrees in the United States is a business degree; the percentage is even·higher if you count the economics majors at schools that don't offer business as a major. "American undergraduates are flocking to business programs, and finding plenty of entry-level opportunities," says Judith Samuelson, executive director of the Aspen Institute's Business and Society Program. But when businesses go hunting for CEOs or managers decades from now, Samuelson adds, "they will say . . . I'm looking for a liberal arts grad."[18]

Businesses want workers who have "the ability to think, the ability to write, the ability to understand the cultural or historical context of whatever business decision they're making," says Rachel Reiser, assistant dean at Boston University's Questrom School of Business.[19] If undergraduates want to find success, they need to master those skills. "We're trying to help them understand there may be so much more to a business education," said Erica Walker, an assistant dean at UC Berkeley's Haas School of Business.[20] The skills of critical thinking, contextualizing problems, and communication are irreplaceable for not only long-term successful careers but also fulfilling lives.

It would be great to say that business schools are offering more and more soft-skill courses because they have spontaneously recognized the intrinsic value of these abilities. Yet, like many things in life, a great part of the effort to offer soft-skill courses came as a response to feedback—in this case, from recruiters.

By all accounts, it seems that students are reaping the benefits of soft-skills training. Many find they fare better in interviews, and do well when asked to perform group work simulations during the application process. Undoubtedly, they also lead more balanced lives.

Countless alumni from Stanford GSB whom I've spoken with reiterate that the soft-skills training was the most valuable part of their education.

Touchy-Feely

Interpersonal Dynamics (or "Touchy-Feely") has been the Stanford Graduate School of Business's most popular elective for forty-five years. I first heard about Touchy-Feely long before I started teaching at GSB, in the form of jokes about MBA students paying for group therapy rebranded as leadership training, to the tune of a hundred grand a year.

The course matches small groups of students with Stanford-trained facilitators. Students engage with topics such as building professional relationships, handling difficult conversations, giving and receiving feedback, and managing conflict and emotions. Facilitators teach students not via role-playing but, rather, by discussing actual events in the students' lives.

As students get to know one another and understand how their peers communicate, the class unpacks conversations in an extremely direct way. Do some students talk over others? Are some deferential or prone to apologizing for taking up space? How is the way they are showing up to the group "landing" with their peers? Through these often difficult conversations, students receive real-time feedback from one another and learn to communicate more effectively.

While this process gives students insight into how their behavior is perceived by others, it doesn't offer them much insight into the intricacies of their own emotional landscapes or how those landscapes influence their behavior. That's where my course comes in. Mindfulness allows us to cultivate skills such as self-awareness. My students also learn strategies such as how to pay attention to their emotional responses to challenging situations. There's nothing wrong with an emotional response, but we need to notice when and why we feel strong emotions, so we can manage our responses to them in the workplace.

While Stanford has been a leader in the teaching of "touchy-feely" skills, other business schools are starting to offer similar classes. At Columbia, students can take courses in the school's Program on Social Intelligence, which offers courses in persuasive speaking and "Action Learning" outings (in which students go off campus to places such as the New York City Fire Department's Randall's Island training facility to practice problem solving and teamwork). Students at Columbia can also take a course in developing personally as leaders, focusing on setting goals and creating a leadership style while also managing expectations and stress.

The first in-depth conversation I had about the impact of Stanford's Touchy-Feely course, and its program overall, was with Bill Park, CEO of Deepdyve and a GSB alumnus. Park felt strongly that Touchy-Feely was the most useful class he and many of his Young Presidents' Organization (YPO) buddies had taken, and as a CEO, he was ahead of the curve in implementing a policy of not quantifying work and sick time—letting his employees take the vacation they wanted, of whatever length they wanted, if they had filled their roles at work. He also developed a personal business plan exercise, the premise of which was the need to be as thoughtful and deliberate about relationships and time *outside* work as those *at* work. And all this exploration for Park was born out of his continuing to apply the insights he had gained through Touchy-Feely, with the added boost from the mindfulness practice he picked up years later.

In fact, it was Park and some other GSB alumni I spoke with who felt that the business school would benefit from layering mindfulness into my Group Dynamics course, to help students learn these skills even better. And it turned out they were right: early on in teaching the course, through papers and in-class discussion, I found that the students were putting together what they'd learned in Touchy-Feely with what they were learning in my class. Park was of the mind that these two together were, in fact, the secret sauce for effective leadership and well-being.

This got me interested in learning more about Touchy-Feely, so I went to Gary Dexter, one of the full-time Touchy-Feely lecturers who I knew was interested in mindfulness. He made the point that if TF is *inter*personal dynamics and mindfulness is *intra*personal dynamics, then mindfulness can be seen as the foundation for interpersonal work. While mindfulness is very much an interpersonal practice, too, I got his point: in this new postmodern, Americanized version of mindfulness, which is about the quiet individual with his or her breath, it is very much an intrapersonal endeavor.

Today, many high-powered executives have begun to recognize the value of soft skills and they are leading industry change by example. In 2016 Arianna Huffington left the *Huffington Post* to start her new company, Thrive, popularizing the notion of the third metric, "a third measure of success that goes beyond the two metrics of money and power, and consists of four pillars: well-being, wisdom, wonder, and giving."[21] And Richard Branson of Virgin Atlantic, Jeff Weiner of LinkedIn, and Marc Benioff at Salesforce are also at the forefront of this change.

It has become clear that the American workplace doesn't function as it should, and that people are unhappy, unhealthy, and in need of a change. It is time to start discussing soft skills as the gateway to the change we need. Because if we develop skills that go beyond interpersonal dynamics and into self-reflection, we can heal both the toxic workplace and ourselves.

2

Full-Catastrophe Working

A NEW BRANCH OF MEDICINE KNOWN AS BEHAVIORAL MEDICINE . . .
BELIEVES THAT MENTAL AND EMOTIONAL FACTORS, THE WAYS IN WHICH
WE THINK AND BEHAVE, CAN HAVE A SIGNIFICANT EFFECT, FOR BETTER
OR WORSE, ON OUR PHYSICAL HEALTH AND ON OUR CAPACITY TO RE-
COVER FROM ILLNESS AND INJURY.

—Jon Kabat-Zinn[1]

Mindfulness expert Jon Kabat-Zinn wrote these words in his classic 1990 book *Full Catastrophe Living*. Today, the "mind-body
connection," as it is popularly referred to, is nothing new, but more
than twenty-five years ago, the program of mindfulness that Kabat-
Zinn introduced to the world was not widely understood. In fact,
many of its early adapters were people who suffered from chronic
pain, desperate to try anything that would offer some relief. Luckily
for them, Kabat-Zinn was no quack. The program, now known as
mindfulness-based stress reduction, or MBSR, was based on solid evidence from the first academic studies of mindfulness, which evaluated its impact on chronic pain.

The participants in those studies (and the millions of readers who made Kabat-Zinn's book a bestseller) experienced the power of mindfulness firsthand. By paying attention, they saw how so much of the experience they didn't want (their pain) was the not wanting itself, and how, conversely, they could make things better by just not making things worse than they already were. In other words, they learned to pay attention in ways that transformed the way they felt physical pain.

In the decades since *Full Catastrophe Living* debuted, the interest in mindfulness has grown exponentially. If you are a research geek, you could keep yourself busy for years reading up on the 325,000 studies on mindfulness that have come out in the past few decades. As of 2014, the National Institutes of Health had spent $92.9 million funding mindfulness research—and the topic has only become hotter in the years since then. Jon Kabat-Zinn's work was just the tip of the iceberg: mindfulness has gone mainstream, and its proven benefits are attracting attention in the business world. Today, you'll find references to mindfulness everywhere, from *Wall Street Journal* headlines to Fortune 500 company retreats. Familiarity with mindfulness and compassion has even become a recruiting advantage: my students tell me it's not unusual to be asked about mindfulness in a first-round job interview, and some companies are using it as a selection criterion.

Thanks to all this research and interest, we now have a wealth of quantitative data that offer evidence of the practical real-world benefits of mindfulness. And we know that the same mechanism that allows for relief from chronic physical pain can also offer relief from the chronic mental pain and stress of work. Paying attention to the hurt that runs through our days—the feelings of insecurity and exclusion, the moments of panic or boredom, all the annoyance, embarrassment, shame, frustration, and rushing from one thing to another (what Kabat-Zinn means by a "full catastrophe")—rather than trying to avoid it or compartmentalize it is how we begin to integrate mindfulness training into our work.

Mindful attention is predicated on two factors: attitude and intention. The attitude we're looking for is open and curious, maybe even tinged with a sense of humor. The intention reaches deep into the very core of ourselves, but it starts on the surface with the modest yet life-changing intention to pay attention to how we're feeling (we'll get into more detail on intention-setting on page 88). Because so much of the pain of work hinges on our avoidance of it (the pain, the work, or both), this is not always easy to do. But the only way to change our experience is to face it.

How Mindfulness Can Lower Your Stress Level

In 2009, Elizabeth Blackburn at the University of California at San Francisco won the Nobel Prize in Physiology or Medicine for her discovery of telomerase, the enzyme that replenishes the protective cap on DNA, the telomere, which is the compound structure at the end of a chromosome. As we age, our telomeres shrink. Because telomeres protect our DNA strands from becoming frayed as they (and we) age, telomere health is regarded as a critical component of longevity.[2]

Today Elissa Epel,[3] also at UCSF, is studying the link between telomeres, aging, and stress. In 2004 she conducted a mindfulness study with a group of high-stress participants: mothers caring for chronically ill children. In the study, some mothers were offered a meditation intervention, and others were not. Those who did not meditate reported feeling more stressed than the meditating mothers and had shorter telomere lengths and lower levels of telomerase than the mothers who meditated. In fact, telomeres in the more frazzled moms showed ten years of aging more than those in their less-stressed counterparts. The takeaway from this study is that not only can meditation help you feel less stressed, but it can actually protect the brain from the damaging effects of stress, which include accelerated aging.

The Real-World Benefits of Mindfulness

Mindfulness may have gone mainstream decades ago, but most people still equate mindfulness practice with something done in private. Yet, just as "work" doesn't exist as a separate category opposed to "life," becoming a more mindful, compassionate person is not in opposition to being a successful, respected professional.

In fact, mindfulness is an immensely practical skill. The human mind is designed to be very active, and our attention strays almost constantly between thoughts, sensations, emotional states, and external stimuli. This is completely normal—it is, in fact, an evolutionary imperative. We need to be able to track what is going on in the world around us. Back in the day, our survival and not getting munched by a predator depended on it: if humans did not keep tabs on the actions of the animals and other humans in their environment, they wouldn't make it to see another day.

Today, the way many of us are in the habit of paying attention isn't as much about safety as about habituation. Over the past few years, I have become used to checking my phone and e-mail several times an hour, and now, when I'm trying to finish a task at my computer, I'll find myself doing it without having made a conscious choice to do so. Of course, it doesn't help that the technology we use was developed specifically to make ongoing bids for our attention, to addict us to the hit of dopamine (the same thing that makes us enjoy food, drugs, and sex) we get when we look at our e-mail or social media yet one more time. But when we start to pay more attention to this habit, we become aware of what our minds are up to. The definition of mindfulness, in its most basic terms, is the intentional use of attention. When we are not aware of where we are placing our attention, we find ourselves at the whim of our thoughts and emotions. This, in turn, colors our interpretation of the world around us and influences the decisions we make.

The good news is that we can be trained in mindfulness, and with practice, we can choose where we place our attention at any given moment. No matter what technique is used—whether it's returning one's attention to the breath, to a physical object, to a visualized object, to physical sensations in the body, or even to a mantra as in Transcendental Meditation—all mindfulness meditation is about training the mind to be where we choose it to be and noticing when it has strayed, so we can bring it back once again. In the process of doing this, we rewire the brain so that over time we become less likely to fall victim to unwanted thought or behavior patterns. This ability to reshape our neural circuitry is known as neuroplasticity.

This process may seem simple enough, but once you try it, you will quickly see it is quite challenging. Eventually, by continuously paying attention to the experience we are having with an attitude of non-judgment, we become more aware of ourselves, the people around us, and our environment. With practice, the neural pathways of the brain wire new patterns that help us focus and that increase our capacity for enacting our purpose, staying on task, being creative, and making better decisions.

The Neuroscience of Mindfulness

We know through the use of fMRI studies that mindfulness practices stimulate changes in the brain. Research has revealed that mindfulness meditation increases our gray matter density in the regions of the brain linked with learning, memory, emotion regulation, and empathy.[4]

Regular mindfulness meditation results in decentering and reperceiving, qualities that are associated with psychological thriving. *Decentering* means participating in the world without being locked into our own perspective in ways that are invisible to us. In other words, we can participate in a situation without making it all about us. *Reperceiving*, another word for this experience of decentering, is our ability to see what is going on in a situation without the layers of interpretation, assumption, or storytelling we use to attribute meanings that may or may not be accurate. Other capacities that are improved with mindfulness include:

- Response to chronic stress
- Response to chronic pain
- Focus
- Productivity
- Behavior change
- Empathic accuracy (reading other people's emotional experience correctly)
- Meta-cognition (being aware of and understanding what we are thinking)

Three Kinds of Mindfulness

In one of my favorite episodes[5] of the show *Curb Your Enthusiasm*, Larry David offers his friend and houseguest Leon Black a tip for an upcoming job interview:

LD: You're going to go in, he'll be up here [gestures with one hand above his head], okay; you're down here [holds the other hand at abdomen level], right? He's on top, he's asking you the questions.
LB: Uh huh.
LD: And then, all of a sudden, the interview starts, he asks some questions, you answer some questions, then you start asking *him* the questions, and you flip it. [Switches top and bottom hands.] Now he's trying to impress you.
LB: Turn that shit around on him.
LD: Turn that shit around.

This is what mindfulness helps us do: turn the tables on our thoughts and feelings. When we pay attention, we flip the dialogue: we're the ones asking the questions. We're gaining awareness of what's really going on. We will still have shitty thoughts sometimes, say shitty things, feel shitty, but when we pay attention and see clearly, we can truly turn things around. When we are mindful, it becomes easier to remember our intentions and question the status quo. And ultimately, it helps us find a better way to respond.

There are different types of mindfulness, and a variety of styles of practice used to develop it. For the purposes of this book, we're going to concentrate on three types of mindfulness training: embodiment, meta-cognition, and focus; and we'll look at how we can realistically integrate these practices into the workday.

EMBODIMENT

Like many performers, world-renowned concert pianist Steven Osborne suffers from stage fright. In an interview with journalist John Lahr for *The New Yorker*, Osborne said that despite its nearly debilitating physiological effects, which include "sweating, confusion, and the loss of language,"[6] he declines to use substances, such as prescription medication or alcohol, to mitigate the anxiety. As he explained to Lahr, "[M]usic is an embodied experience; you're making emotional experiences come alive for other people, through your body. If you screen off that side of yourself, it means there's a whole range of emotions which become unavailable to you." Osborne went on to describe how he has trained his mind to get through these moments, and says he offers the same training to his students.

Osborne may be more open about his stage fright than other performers, but he is far from alone. According to the United Kindgom's *Telegraph*,[7] a 2012 study of orchestras in Germany found that one-third of musicians used Valium or beta-blockers to manage their stage fright.

But you don't have to be a musician performing in front of thousands to suffer from performance anxiety. In fact, public speaking—something that most of us in the working world face at some point—ranks higher than death on some surveys about the things people fear most. It is also one of the tasks that researchers use in clinical settings to induce and study stress.

Osborne's observation that every experience is an embodied experience is true for all of us, not just performers who rely on their bodies. In every interaction, we make emotional experiences come alive for the people around us. Those of us who aren't musicians, actors, athletes, or trapeze artists tend to forget this, *especially* at work. We know ourselves primarily as thought havers, and we experience the world through our heads. If we notice our bodies at all, most likely it is when they interrupt our thoughts—in the form of carpel tunnel syndrome, back pain, breast pumping, sore feet, or simply the routine hunger that forces us to stop what we're doing multiple times a day to eat. If we exercise our bodies, we often begrudge the time it takes from other things. Perhaps we "forget" to exercise, or don't bother to because our bodies don't seem as important as what our brains are up to. We forget that the two are connected.

Embodiment, by contrast, is mindfulness of the body. With embodiment, we practice bringing our attention into our bodies, noticing the tension, circulation, pain, pleasure, or just neutral physical experience of, say, our right shoulder, or our abdomen, or the arch of our left foot. We attend to sensations as they occur—cramps, knots, butterflies, queasiness, and all.

At this point, you may reasonably ask: Why would we want to do this? Why, given the imperfections of our mortal human form, the inconvenient, uncomfortable, embarrassing, and at times painful mix of physical reality with which we are afflicted every day, would we want to pay *more* attention to our bodies? Why not less? For those of us who don't use our bodies to earn our keep, aren't bodies just a liability at work? After all, we have to dress them, schlep them, feed them, caffeinate them, hydrate them, relieve them. And for many of us working in physically undemanding jobs, our bodies don't seem to give much in return—so, for the most part, we're in the habit of ignoring them. Embodiment, therefore, lets us take a closer look and see what we've been missing. Both science and traditional wisdom tell us that doing so is important, and that there are ways we can flip the dialogue to see our bodies as a resource rather than a drag.

We cause ourselves a lot of unnecessary suffering when our minds are missing in action—rehashing the past, predicting the future, narrating the present—and our bodies are the quickest, surest way back to the present moment. When we're aware of our physical sensations, we are, by definition, present. The body doesn't speculate or regret, worry or anticipate. As such, it can be our anchor in reality, in the present tense. Mindfulness training starts there. Indeed, our language is full of commonsense phrases suggesting embodiment, from "Get out of your head" and "Check your gut" to "Speak from the heart" and "Take a deep breath" to "Let me catch my breath."

The breath occupies a special place in the canon of mind-body figures of speech, and for good reason (and both mindfulness traditions and modern science agree on this): between the physicality of the body and the immateriality of the mind, the breath lies somewhere in the middle, a bridge from one to the other. A single breath can take us out of our heads for a moment. A single breath, and the attendant shift into the body, gives us a break from the mind's chatter, an opportunity to reset. At the same time, it puts us in a position to see our thoughts and feelings as just thoughts and feelings, not the last word or ultimate truth. Most of the time, we're in the middle of telling ourselves a story about something, and we fully believe it. A single breath can take us out of the story, making us that much less gullible. So, a single breath is an instant perspective changer. We can follow it into our bodies, where we have just enough distance to judge whether our heads are with us (that is, in line with our current intentions and greater purpose) or against us, and to choose which way we want to go from here. And because breathing is not something we need to take time out of our day to do, we can always find our way back to our bodies through the breath.

Imagine this scenario. You are in a meeting and a coworker speaks over you, cutting you off. You may feel annoyed and want to lash out at him, but your boss is also there, and you don't want to look like an overreactive jerk in front of him. After all, it is you who will look bad, not the interrupter. So, you take a few breaths. You feel your heart race and your adrenaline pump, readying you for an act of self-protection. As you breathe, you feel your heartbeat start to slow. Once your body has calmed down, you interject at the next opportunity and make your original point with grace.

One reason that embodiment and learning to focus on the breath are such valuable tools in the workplace is because when we are triggered by stress, we experience a specific cascade of physiological changes. From a neuroscientific perspective, our amygdala, an almond-shaped group of neurons that lies deep in the brain, is where information from emotions is processed. Stimulating the amygdala creates intense emotions: fear, aggression, etc. PET scans show that when we have panic attacks, there is increased blood flow to that region. Yet, just as the amygdala can be trained to react with fear readily, as in the case of trauma or ongoing high stress, it can also be retrained to interpret external and internal stimuli without jumping to a fear response.

When the amygdala is activated by a situation it perceives as a threat, our body responds by increasing muscle tension and speeding up heart rate—which leads to accelerated breathing. This is the classic "fight-or-flight" stress response, the body's way of preparing us to battle it out or flee from a threat. Shallow breaths, in turn, lead to increasing the activation of fear in the brain and body. A 2016 study[8] done by a group of German neuroscientists trained study participants with no prior meditation or yoga experience in simple attention to breath practice for two weeks and then exposed them to upsetting images. When the subjects used mindful breathing techniques while viewing the disturbing images, they were found to have greater subjective success regulating their emotion, which also corresponded significantly with lower amygdala activation.

The more frequently we experience our body's stress response, the more easily we become triggered. Soon the muscle tension and rapid breathing themselves may become danger signals to the amygdala. This is the power of classical conditioning: the association between danger and our body's reaction to danger becomes so strong that, in effect, we take our body's reaction as evidence of danger, just as Pavlov's dogs took the sound of that bell as "evidence" of dinner. As a result, a vicious circle may develop whereby the increased muscle tension and rapid breathing caused by an activated amygdala further activate the amygdala. The farther upstream you can catch yourself reacting to stressful situations, therefore, the easier it will be to calm down. This is why, when I teach mindfulness to veterans with PTSD, I have them focus on detecting the first glimmers of physical symptoms, so that they can employ mindfulness techniques as early as possible. If the person is in a full-blown state of distress, it is much more challenging for him to down-regulate.

If you find yourself getting worked up, as in the interruption example, stewing on it in your corner of the conference room by rehashing all one hundred previous times this particular colleague interrupted you, you are taking yourself out of the meeting mentally and also guaranteeing that you are going to need longer to get your mind back online for service. If you catch yourself reacting, right after the interruption occurs, take a few breaths mindfully; this will prevent the escalation from happening in the first place, and the recovery will be shorter, too. We can use the association between relaxed muscles, slower breath, and the absence of a threat to reverse the cycle—in short, we can use embodiment to physically flip the script.

Another way the breath can impact our mental state is through sighing. Sighing is the body's natural way of hitting the Reset button. It is a common coping response for people with high anxiety, panic disorder, or post-traumatic stress disorder. Intentional deep breathing mimics the benefits of automatic sighing. A 2016 study in Belgium[9] on the "psychophysiology of emotions" compared the effects of the respiratory system on the way emotions show up in the body. The objective of the study was to clarify the ways in which deep breathing and holding one's breath impacted psychological and physical relief in response to stress exposure.

Researchers recruited thirty-four subjects between the ages of eighteen and thirty-one who did not have a history of psychological diagnosis or exposure to physical or mental trauma and measured their baseline respiration. The participants were then shown images that connoted danger, safety, or ambiguity. Depending on which group they had been assigned to, they were given instructions to breathe deeply, hold their breath, or breathe normally. The researchers found that both deep breaths and spontaneous sighs engendered physiological relief. The held breath did not have this impact. Interestingly, the deep breaths were associated with psychological relief, but the sighs impacted only the physiological and not the psychological (self-reported subjective experience of relief). When you take your deep breaths, if you feel yourself starting to get agitated, do it mindfully, paying attention to the physical sensations of breathing. And when a coworker sighs loudly, recognize that it might have more to do with him coping with stress than with an irritation you might be misattributing to his situation.

Another reason to practice embodiment is that, as contrary as it may seem to the way we typically think about emotion, our bodies are *where* we feel. Emotions may seem like a liability much of the time, especially at work, but in fact, our emotions are an asset: they contain information that can help us interpret and address a situation in which something isn't right, in the workplace and elsewhere—if we are paying attention. When we pay attention to our bodies, we can catch emotional information as it heads upstream, before it hijacks our whole system. Once again, we're flipping the dialogue. Embodiment can also be thought of as an extension of the idea of knowing something in your gut.

And in fact, recent research has shown that feelings can "begin" in the gut. Indeed, our referring to the gut as our "second brain" comes from the fact that it has more than two hundred million neurons and contains three-quarters of the body's immune cells. The gut and the brain communicate in both directions—brain to gut but also gut to brain. These two regions have multiple systems for this communication—the endocrine, neuronal, and immune pathways—so if the text is missed, a fax or phone call can make its way without interruption.[10] The gut has a strong influence on the emotions we experience. For example, taking courses of probiotics has been shown to alter anxiety and depression. Serotonin, the neurotransmitter that allows nerves to communicate with one another and is involved in mood regulation, is far more predominant in the gut and digestive tract than in the brain (between 80 and 90 percent more).

If we let them, our bodies can also connect us to other people, since the human body is a major part of what we have in common with our fellow human beings. Our bodies and the pleasure and pain that come with them—their attendant aches and illnesses, their needs and indignities, the impossibility of having the body we want, the fear of losing it, our vulnerability in the day-to-day, the kindnesses we have received to make it this far and that we'll need again when we are sick and dying, and the very ways we fight our bodies or pretend they don't exist—as human beings, we share all of this.

Finally, when we are not present in our bodies at work, we miss out on a source of pleasure. It's human nature to notice the pain more, but with reminders and practice, we can take joy throughout the day in the simple, reliable pleasures of having a body. Mindfulness through embodiment gives us the power, in effect, to magnify the little things that we may be in the habit of overlooking because we believe they're insignificant. Embodying pleasures such as sitting when we've been standing for too long, or standing up and stretching when we've been sitting for too long; holding a new pen with a particularly comfortable ergonomic grip; laughing hard when something's funny; eating when we're hungry; drinking when we're thirsty; perking up with caffeine when we're drowsy; the relative quiet of the office after a morning with screaming kids; slipping out of uncomfortable shoes under our desk or not wearing uncomfortable shoes in the first place—every day, no matter how lousy it is otherwise, affords us countless opportunities like these to feel good, and the body is where we feel it. In fact, as we've all experienced when we finally feel better after an illness, every part of our body that does *not* hurt is a cause for celebration and a source of joy waiting to be accessed at any time.

This is the purpose of physical rituals in any religious tradition, from bowing or chanting to the smell of incense or a sprinkle of water: repeated, embodied actions that move us beyond our limited, head-centric perspective and thus expand our sense of self and experience. You may not be allowed to light a candle in your office, and you may not want to, but both science and tradition are replete with rituals you can adapt to the workplace. The act of hanging our coat and emptying our bag when we arrive in the morning, of laying out our materials on a conference room desk, of docking and silencing our cell phone, of adjusting from a seated to a standing desk—we can use all these behavioral routines we insert into our day to recalibrate mentally, to take a moment to anchor our attention in our body.

» Returning Attention to the Body

To help ground ourselves in our body, we can set up prompts to direct our attention where we want it to go. One of my students changed the password on her computer and phone to "BREATHE." When she took a breath upon logging in, she explained, it allowed her to touch base with her intention, so that rather than compulsively checking her e-mail, she could choose to work on projects that mattered to her. A prompt tied to a habitual event (logging into your computer, taking your seat in a meeting, answering the phone) can remind you to be in your body at a critical moment.

Here are three simple techniques.

1. **Take a Breath.** You'll never forget to breathe, but you will forget to notice that you're breathing. Whole days go by without our paying attention to, let alone appreciating, the pleasure of a single breath. So, wherever you are, whether sitting or standing, stop for a moment and take a full breath, feeling the air go through your nostrils and into your lungs, contracting your diaphragm, and then hold it for a few moments, letting your stomach puff out. Then exhale fully, visualizing that as you breathe out the air, you are also breathing out any stress, anxiety, anger, and feelings of being overwhelmed. Feel whatever you are carrying inside you exit your body, making space for a new full breath. Do this three times, and take your time.

2. **Breath Meditation.** A step beyond just taking three deep breaths is to intentionally focus on your breath as a sort of miniature meditation. As you breathe in and out, put your attention on your breath, on the sensation of breathing. Feel the air go in and out of your body, and when your mind wanders— and it will—shift your attention back to your breath. Don't filter any thoughts or manipulate the experience. Just let the thoughts settle on their own as you continue to focus on the simple act of breathing slowly in and out.

3. **Do a Body Scan.** Bring your attention to the top of your head. Slowly move it down your body—through your face, neck, torso, legs, and to your feet. Then move back up. Repeat. When your mind wanders—and it will—return your attention to feeling the sensations in the various parts of your body through which you are sweeping your attention. The purpose of this exercise

is not only to help you get back into your body, but also to collect information and get curious about what you usually avoid.
If there is pain, can you look into it? What are the sensations
made of? Notice your aversion to discomfort. Can you accept
the discomfort? How might your awareness of discomfort
inform your experience of work? When you ignore or avoid
these sensations, are you more likely to express the pain in
the wrong context (e.g., by making bad decisions, by snapping
at someone)?

META-COGNITION

A second kind of mindfulness, meta-cognition, is the practice of
knowing what we are experiencing while we are experiencing it. Don't
worry. It's less trippy or philosophical than it might sound. Right now,
can you see these words on the page of this book (or e-reader), or hear
them being spoken in audio, and be aware that you are reading at the
same time? Can you sit while also feeling the chair supporting you?
Can you know what you are thinking about? If you were born after
1980, you might think of this ability as the phone camera in your
mind, the part of you that recognizes an experience as worthy of a
social media post (or not). Meta-awareness is "So, *that* happened" in
the present tense: "So, *this* is what's happening."

The Buddha is said to have been asked by a skeptical attendee of
one of his talks what the big fuss was about. His answer was that
his monastics knew they were standing while they were standing,
sitting while they were sitting, eating while they were eating, and
walking while they were walking. By extension, we should know we are
e-mailing while we are e-mailing, driving (not texting!) while we are
driving, feeling angry or jealous or what have you when we are feeling
angry, jealous, or what have you. This sounds so obvious that it's almost silly.

Yet it is not.

If we pay attention, we see that we are rarely aware of what we're doing when we're doing it. One of the inevitable side effects of paying more attention to what's happening is noticing how hard it is to *really* pay attention, and how often we don't. With practice, our ability to iterate attention between the thing we're aware of and awareness itself increases. Monks and nuns get very good at sustaining meta-awareness because they practice the skill a lot and also have rituals throughout the day (pausing for prayer before eating, for example) that help them keep their meta-awareness going. But we nonmonastics, too, can learn to build ritual reminders into our daily routines.

At the Yale Center for Emotional Intelligence,[11] director Marc Brackett and his colleagues developed a pioneering program for schools that instructs students and teachers alike in using meta-moments, among other practices, to increase their emotional intelligence. Participants learn to reflect, self-regulate, and manage challenging emotional experiences. They are then asked to think of how they could act in a way that honors both who they are and what they want for their community. Teenage students plagued with stress over college applications or grades or interpersonal problems say that meta-moments help them remember to have perspective. Even young students can understand and benefit. According to one kindergartner, "When we're driving in the car, sometimes [my siblings] will be arguing, and that makes me feel frustrated. So I say, 'Let's take a meta-moment.'" My own kids will suggest breathing exercises to me or my husband when they see that we are starting to freak out due to stress. And recently I've begun initiating silence contests on long car rides when my entire family is freaking out.

On the whole, Brackett and his team have found that the meta-moment practice improved the behavior and wellness of students. For example, low-income schools that have implemented the program have seen their suspension rates fall by 60 percent.[12]

Twenty-five hundred years after the Buddha came up with his program, research findings like these validate what all the fuss is about, the freedom we gain by taking a moment. A moment of meta-awareness contains the possibility of thinking, feeling, and doing according to our best intentions. Seeing something in a different light, not getting sucked in, telling the truth even when we're ashamed, delaying gratification (and appreciating when we are truly gratified), imagining how the person across from us is experiencing this moment, not yelling or being defensive, finding (as a friend's mother likes to say) "another way to feel," and understanding what's *really* going on—all these start with a meta-moment.

One exercise I employ when I teach my students about meta-moments is the metaphor of a balcony overlooking our emotional landscape. I didn't come up with this on my own; I borrowed it from Kennedy School professor Ronald Heifetz and his colleagues Alexander Grashow and Marty Linsky.[13] As coauthors of the book *The Practice of Adaptive Leadership*, they explain that the perspective we get from "stepping onto the balcony" is an incredibly empowering form of meta-awareness. We can be above the fray and objectively view our own "tuning," that is, all the aspects of our identities and experiences that influence how we see the world: gender, race, age, religion, and our personal history and triggers. Triggers are our sensitivities, or hot buttons. According to Heifitz, Grashaw, and Linsky, effective leaders know their own tuning and hot buttons so well that they don't fly off the handle when those buttons are pressed. In my teaching, I have connected these concepts of tuning and triggers with the data gleaned through applied mindfulness practice. While the patterns that unfold in our bodies (our tuning and triggers) are highly individual, the ways in which we can recognize and deal with the information translates across people.

We categorize people and facts in order to be efficient, to make sense of them. But the categories we use also have negative consequences—

for example, when we stereotype people who are not in our social in-group. According to Renee Navarro, UCSF's vice chancellor for diversity and outreach (who leads UCSF's initiative to address unconscious bias), we are more likely to enact an unconscious bias when we are stressed, under pressure, or multitasking. And let's face it, aren't reacting to time pressure and multitasking pretty much our default ways of being while we are at work?

"Most of us believe that we are ethical and unbiased. We imagine we're good decision makers, able to objectively size up a job candidate or a venture deal and reach a fair and rational conclusion that's in our, and our organization's, best interests," writes Harvard University researcher Mahzarin Banaji in the *Harvard Business Review*.[14] "But more than two decades of research confirms that, in reality, most of us fall woefully short of our inflated self-perception."

Interestingly, a number of studies suggest that mindfulness practice can reduce implicit or unconscious bias. For example, after listening to a ten-minute guided mindfulness meditation, white participants in a study were less likely than those in the control group to link black or old faces with negative words. The reason, scholars suggest, is that mindfulness takes us out of automatic responses, the autopilot that lets us employ unchecked stereotypes. Social psychology researchers Adam Leuke and Bryan Gibson have found that, with even this brief guided meditation, both age and race discrimination can be decreased. So it may well be that in hiring processes, slowing down and allowing for less automaticity in responding could go a long way.

I often ask my students to share times when they were triggered at work and, using the awareness of meta-moments, to describe what I call their "tells" (yes, referencing poker). Here is one student's example of being triggered:

In my old job at a private equity firm in New York, I was working on a project for one of the companies we were invested in. Normally, the partner with whom I was working supported my ideas and allowed me to control my own direction on much of my work. In this case, though, he was being extremely domineering. He kept thinking of new analyses we should conduct and variables to look at. He kept switching the questions we should be answering. He kept telling me to do my work in a slightly different way. The management style was so volatile and intrusive that I found it very difficult to keep my cool. I remember a heat in my chest, which seemed to vibrate with increasing intensity as I became more and more upset. Every time I'd go back to my desk, I would silently scream. I didn't end up saying anything; I just ended up becoming increasingly frustrated until we were finally done and the partner left.

An important need this situation points to is my opinion being respected and valued in the workplace. I felt like I had no agency or control over what I was doing; questions were being asked, then changed or reframed once I tried to answer them. The lack of efficiency in this process also triggered me. Finally, I value consistency in a work environment. This partner had previously treated my work with respect and given me a lot of independence. This behavior was an unwelcome departure from that style of management. What's more, this behavior was not typical of other partners at the firm, which increased the feeling of mistreatment and inconsistency.

And another:

This past summer, before starting at the GSB, I worked at a private equity firm. I had very little spreadsheet experience going into the summer, as I had spent the last two years at law school and the year before at a nonprofit. A few days after my internship began, the work started piling on. I had about three assignments I was working on simultaneously when the CFO asked me to step into his office so he could give me another assignment. The assignment was to update a spreadsheet tracking the deals that the firm had seen over the past month.

As he began describing the assignment, I realized that he was assuming that I had far more technical knowledge than I actually had. I interrupted him a few times to explain that I had very limited experience with the computer program, but he would just offer a short explanation and continue. The instruction continued for some time as I hastily took notes. After around fifteen minutes, the meeting was over and I found myself back in my office. Reflecting on the assignment I was just given, I realized that I understood about 5 percent of what I was supposed to do and that the CFO did not seem like he wanted to be bothered until the assignment was finished.

Once I realized this, I felt a rush of anxiety. I started sweating and felt a pulsating feeling in my chest and stomach. I spent almost half an hour trying to calm myself down. While this was a particularly intense situation, milder versions of this feeling happen to me quite often. These episodes are usually accompanied by similar physical "tells"—a pulsating feeling that begins in my chest and makes its way down to my stomach.

After reflecting on these episodes, I have realized that my underlying need to be in control is what often causes me to be triggered. Whenever I am given a task, in order to feel that I am in control, I must have an understanding of the steps required to complete the task and confidence that I will have the time to complete these steps. In other words, when I am confronted with a problem, if I do not immediately have a blueprint and schedule for how to solve the problem, I feel that I have lost control.

Suffice it to say that simply noticing what's happening in the moment is a great leap forward in dealing with conflict at work and in life.

Psychologists call it "dereification," which means to make something less concrete or real. In this case, the "somethings" we're concerned with are our thoughts, feelings, and perceptions as they unfold, which we dereify simply by recognizing them for what they are: thoughts, feelings, and perceptions—as opposed to, say, believing that our every thought is the last word and ultimate truth. From a neuroscientific perspective, thoughts are electrochemical activity in the brain, coupled with autonomic arousal in the body—either way, they're natural, transitory phenomena emerging from our more or less adaptive systems of response. The meta-moment gives us time and space to observe what's happening in our minds and bodies, and to suspend our beliefs. Research has shown that our ability to view our emotional reactions from a more objective viewpoint is a critical determinant of whether our reflection on emotion is constructive or whether it degenerates into maladaptive rumination—or, as one of my students so eloquently put it, "recycling thoughts."

What power! You get to decide whether that self-flagellating thought looping in your head is true or not. You get to pause just long enough to see that your paranoid suspicions are just paranoid suspicions, and then go on to consider other reasons for your coworker to be acting that way. You see an urge as just an urge, something that will pass if you let it, not something you necessarily have to do.

This goes for other people's thoughts, feelings, and perceptions, too. They might not be right about everything. On the other hand, they might be more (or equally) right about something than you first realized. What a relief! By observing what's happening objectively, you don't have to fight with everybody (if only in your head) all the time. Meditation teacher Michele McDonald[15] once noted, at the beginning of a weeklong silent retreat, how much of our "personality" is just habits of thought, feeling, and perception, and how many of our thoughts, feelings, and perceptions boil down to "Why can't everyone be more like me?" If we could see this, and if we could choose, wouldn't we choose another way to be? In the meta-moment, we can.

FOCUS

Focus is the ability to place attention where we want it. It is also the intentional use of attention, which, as we know, is the very definition of mindfulness. There are different degrees of focus, of course. A narrow, or laser, focus is an intense honing in, through a smaller aperture. We use this type of narrowed attention to execute a single task—to type up a report perhaps, or to prepare for an interview. There is also a broader, panoramic aperture, a wider kind of focus, where we take in not just the details but the context, the broader landscape. We use this type of attention to recognize the connections between ideas or data points that may not be obvious, which can come in handy when you're attending a conference and listening to various presentations. All types of focus are extremely valuable, especially when we have the awareness to choose what type of attention to "pay" depending on the situation.

Focus is best titrated, or adjusted, and this skill of titrating attention can be improved with practice. Allowing yourself to remain focused but also relaxed is the best way to engender a "flow" state (which, by definition, requires engagement but not being stressed). Often, when people start meditating or integrating mindfulness training into their everyday lives, they try too hard to focus on being aware, and the mind then jumps around as a reaction. Or they don't focus enough, and their mind slips away and they forget to stay aware. I had a student who would get up and leave a meditation session, becoming embroiled in another task, and who would then realize, after some time, that he had ended his session: he just reacted in a knee-jerk fashion to the thought that something needed doing. This isn't to say that we should never interrupt our focus to respond to urgent needs. It is about making a choice to do this. When we practice mindfulness, we can see that it is possible to carry the thread of awareness throughout our experience of the day. And as the traditional metaphor goes, we use our intention to keep the watchman (watchperson) of mindfulness by our side throughout the day.

The benefit of focusing our attention is that when our larger goal or purpose is clear, we know where to put our attention, focusing on the right things. We can tackle the task at hand instead of focusing on, say, a negative reaction from a colleague or the emotions we feel as a result of that reaction. If our purpose is squarely in mind and we are able to focus on that higher purpose, we don't get carried away by emotions or unwanted events.

Applying the practice of creating rituals, we can devise prompts that remind us to be aware of our focus. Prompts to focus, when intentionally planted at specific intervals in our day, grab our attention and pull us out of autopilot so that we don't resort to the mental shortcuts we unconsciously deploy in order to conserve energy.

For example, a great way to create focus is to select an activity you know for certain you'll do, such as brushing your teeth. Then, when you come to that activity, it will serve as a reminder for you to pay attention. You can use transitional moments as prompts or physical activity. For me, turning off my Wi-Fi or setting one of those nifty visual timers, to remind me to keep at whatever I'm working on, is very helpful. If you work at Starbucks, pulling shots to make a cup of coffee can be a prompt. Making notes in a patient's chart, if you work in health care, or sanitizing your hands between patients, can also serve. If you're a teacher of children, your prompt could be the bell starting class. If you work in an office, it could be when you walk into the conference room for a meeting. In short, your prompt should be an everyday moment that triggers you to pay attention, know your intention, and stay on task.

Time management really comes down to attention management and knowing where to place your focus. It's not easy—I know I always have the temptation to knock out a few e-mails as soon as I turn on my computer, and the next thing I know, it's almost lunchtime. When you first walk into your office or turn on your computer or begin your shift, do it with great intentionality. Which item on your endless list of tasks will have the highest impact? Do you really need to be at that meeting or on that call? From there, you can move into energy management, which is assessing what is depleting versus uplifting you.

Creating Prompts

Experiment with selecting activities or tasks that you will do with as full a presence as possible. When composing an e-mail, for example, you could focus on that e-mail only, instead of scanning your in-box every time you hear a ping. When your mind wanders from the task, gently return it. Over time, consider adding more prompts to your daily routine.

Take an inventory of your daily task list. Identify one or two activities you could use as an awareness prompt. When you encounter your prompt, practice bringing your attention to what you are doing in that moment and return your attention to it over and over each time it wanders off. You can think of each of these returns to the task at hand as a "rep," just like a bicep curl would be in the gym if you were developing your upper-body strength. Take inventory of your breath and how your body feels.

Pay attention to how you feel when you are able to redirect your thoughts from the many places they may be wandering and back to your current task. When we see what we were feeling underneath the attempt to distract ourselves, often it is anxiety or discomfort. If we could just feel this feeling we wouldn't have to hide from it and get into the cycle of procrastination that leads to our feeling more anxiety and discomfort.

Remember the principle of *dampa sum*: good in the beginning, good in the middle, good in the end? Mindfulness is a good intention to have, a useful skill to practice, and it offers a multitude of benefits. Don't be too hard on yourself if reading this chapter hasn't resulted in nonjudgmental awareness of your difficult feelings or wandering attention overnight. Beyond helping us better understand our emotions and focus with intention, mindfulness also has a reciprocal relationship with purpose, which we will discuss in the next chapter. Being mindful helps you know your purpose, and knowing your purpose can become an anchor in your mindfulness practice.

3

On Purpose (with a Capital *P*)

THOSE WHO HAVE A "WHY" TO LIVE CAN BEAR WITH ALMOST ANY "HOW."
—Viktor Frankl, *Man's Search for Meaning*

The Brookline home stands on the corner of two quiet residential streets, a charming Victorian with gray paint and yellow trim, and homey touches throughout that belie the professional architect who has lived here for decades. Light pours in from the sun porch behind my seat at the dining room table. There are four of us: Michael "Misha" Kraus, architect and Holocaust survivor; next to him his wife, Ilana, a doctor and kick-ass grandma; Michael Grodin of the Boston Center for Refugee Health and Human Rights, pioneer in the field of resilience and also known as Dr. G; and me. I was thirty-two at the time, apprenticing with Dr. G; Misha and Ilana were in their eighties; Dr. G about halfway in between.

Misha was telling us about running the journal *Kamarad* in Czechoslovakia as a child. It was unusual for boys between the ages of twelve and fourteen to write for a publication, let alone be in charge of one, but such were the circumstances at the Terezín concentration camp. Now Misha laid out copies of *Kamarad* on the white tablecloth for us to see. (Originals that survived are archived in Israel.) I couldn't read the articles, as they were written in Czech, but Misha explained that most of them were fantasies, intricate stories set in the Wild West, as far away from the Czechoslovakia in the early 1940s as their writers could imagine. There was a comic series about a race car driver, and a column about soccer. Misha spoke with a combination of pride, reverence, and sadness about how the articles had provided an escape for readers and writers alike. Bold and colorful, the illustrations spoke for themselves.

The writing was fiction, but the project and its attendant problems—sourcing materials (paper was particularly scarce then) and writing in crowded, noisy, gravely dangerous conditions—were real. For the team of contributors, their purpose in doing it was real, too: the act of working on the publication offered them something more than merely surviving, if they survived, something better than suffering while they suffered, something of theirs that would live on after them if they died.

When I met him seven decades later, Misha was still going to work every day, now as an architect (principal emeritus) at one of Boston's oldest firms. He has said that the survivor speaking circuit never felt quite right for him. Talking about his experiences during the war was agitating, possibly even retraumatizing, though he appreciated that for others it was different. For his part, he was eager to have the story of *Kamarad* and its message of purpose make its way into the world. He wanted us to understand that meaning is not a luxury for lucky, safe, well-fed, well-paid, comfortable, and not-too-busy people with nothing more urgent to worry about. Nor is it a medal for exceptional people or a consolation prize for hard times. Meaning is a human need, and a choice or set of choices everybody can make in any circumstance, at any moment. Literally or figuratively, depending on the situation, purpose is a matter of life and death. As his fellow survivor Victor Frankl wrote in *Man's Search for Meaning*, "Life is never made unbearable by circumstances, but only by lack of meaning and purpose."

Purpose is something we do, something we create—not something we buy, inherit, achieve, or otherwise obtain. Purpose boosts our capacity to make the greatest impact in the work we do, and to connect with other people across cultures and contexts, however powerless or lonely we might feel. We are energized, motivated, and expanded by a sense of purpose.

Purpose could be any direction in which we're heading with some degree of intention, but not every direction should be called a purpose with a capital *P*. We can probably all agree that heading to the 7-Eleven for a cold drink, even if we're really thirsty on a very hot day, does not in itself qualify as a purpose. I am interested in the capital-*P* kind of purpose, which is a far-reaching, steady goal, something personally meaningful and self-transcending that, ideally, shows up in our lives every day. Purpose has impact only if we sincerely care about it, hence the "personally meaningful" part. If I take on my husband's or coworker's purpose because it sounds good or because he thinks I should take it on, I won't benefit from the clarity in orientation and sense of fulfillment that authentic purpose offers. Purpose provides context for our lives; it lends us a perspective that includes more than our individual priorities and problems, wants and needs, pulling us out of myopic tendencies and connecting us with the world around us.

Purpose tends not to show up on people's to-do lists, crammed as those lists usually are with practical tasks. You don't often see "Buy milk, water plants, catch up on e-mails, and make the world a better place" on a Post-it on the fridge. We may think about purpose in passing, or the topic might surface in a deep conversation with a friend, but more often than not, we tend to view purpose as a pipe dream or an "unrealistic" goal we pursued in our early twenties—not something relevant and applicable to our actual, everyday lives. Who has the time for existential questions? We have to get to our kid's doctor's appointment, or the gym, or the grocery store, or work. We may quietly, blindly hope that all our tasks and busyness add up to something greater than the sum of their parts, but we're afraid they might not. Too often, we can't see the connection between the big and little picture, or we just don't have the time to stop and take a breath and ask the question.[*]

Purpose Makes Your Job More Satisfying

At the Yale School of Management, every MBA student takes a class on purpose at work. As Dr. Amy Wrzesniewski teaches it, this course is as beloved as it is mandatory, probably thanks to her special combination of warmth and clarity that puts anxious MBA students at ease. The question at the heart of Wrzesniewski's research,[1] on which the class is based, is: What makes work fulfilling? Given two people in the same position, why will one person find her work more satisfying than the other? Or, to ask a question Wrzesniewski posed in one study, when people are given the same one-paragraph summary about a working person they do not know, why would each person offer a very different interpretation of the stranger's work? If "Mr. A's" work is described as "basically a necessity of life, a lot like sleeping or breathing," would you say it's very important to him, or would you say it's an uninspired "day job" that he doesn't think much about? What factors account for the difference?

---

[*] Here are some arguments for and against to-do lists: www.leahweissphd.com /todo.

Wrzesniewski's answers to these kinds of questions contribute to a growing heap of evidence that individual disposition and personality traits have real implications for how we experience our work. A job itself is neither awesome nor terrible, since the experience we have doing a job depends largely on what we bring to it. Most of us, she has found, see our work as a "job," a way to make money. Some of us have a "career" and focus on advancement over time. Others understand their work as a "calling," that is, socially valuable even if the tasks involved are not always pleasant.

It's my view that over the course of a year or month or day, we might inhabit multiple of these mind-sets. And paying attention to this can help us realize when we are inhabiting a mind-set that is less aligned with our purpose. I don't mean to imply that a job isn't a purpose in itself. If a job enables us to buy food for our family and provide a comfortable place to rest our bodies at night, we are fulfilling a purpose. Still, we can benefit from becoming aware of how we think about our work and deciding if that framework serves us.

According to Wrzesniewski, people who consider their work to be a calling tend to be more satisfied with how they earn a living than those who think of their work as "just" a job. That may not be surprising, but what is surprising is that the difference in these orientations is not simply a function of the kind of work we do or the role we play within an organization. Meaning and satisfaction are not sitting up there in the executive suite, out of reach to all but the biggest cheeses, and a calling isn't built into any one industry. Wrzesniewski has surveyed administrative associates, physicians, nurses, hospital custodial workers, librarians, computer programmers, clerical employees, and zookeepers, and when asked to describe their work, these workers used one of all three labels—job, career, or calling.

For example, in one of Wrzesniewski's groups, she gathered administrative associates of comparable ages, incomes, and education levels.

Nine said they had "jobs," seven felt they had "careers," and eight described their work as a "calling." The related differences in the degree of satisfaction experienced by the workers was real and measurable. The "career" workers stayed in their positions longer than their peers with "jobs," and those with a "calling" missed fewer days of work.

The hospital custodial workers offer another interesting example. Many people use "janitor" as shorthand for a job-job, the quintessential "shitty job" that somebody's gotta do. When Wrzesniewski studied the orientations of hospital janitors, however, she found dramatically different outlooks among people in the exact same role. Some janitors felt they were an essential part of a patient's recovery. They sought out ways to make their work more supportive of the patients' healing, modifying the type and timing of their cleaning to work around patient needs and chatting with the patients in their rooms as they worked. Some of the custodians even kept in touch with patients after they were discharged. These are examples of what scholars call "extra-role behavior," or doing things that fall outside our position's stated duties. This skill, of finding the meaningful, doable actions that make our work purposeful, is central to customizing work and aligning it with our values.

The point of these studies is not to say that janitors and others in low-pay positions should have a positive attitude. It's that many do, and their example is something all of us can learn from. We, too, can bring purpose to our work, no matter how shitty our jobs may feel. We can start doing this immediately. We don't have to wait for work to become meaningful, for some promotion or future career change. We don't have to despair that it never will. We can put our hearts into the thing we're doing right now.

Research shows that there are real, measurable benefits to having a sense of purpose at work. At HopeLab, we conducted a study of the physical and mental benefits of purpose. Steve Cole, professor of medicine, psychiatry, and biobehavioral sciences at the UCLA School of

Medicine and an expert on social genomics (the ways in which our environment and behavior impact the expression of our genes),[2] was in charge of the study. Cole's team found that the benefits of having a sense of purpose in the workplace included:

Occupational identification (how much we define ourselves in terms of the work we do);

A sense of kinship and community with colleagues;

A feeling that work is purposeful and important to society;

A sense of occupational importance due to value alignment;

A sense of purpose toward something larger than oneself; and

Trivial and unpleasant tasks becoming infused with larger meaning and significance.

This greater sense of meaning in life was associated with:

Greater life satisfaction;

Greater psychological well-being;

Greater positive affect;

Greater emotional ties with others (connection);

Less psychological distress;

Less negative affect; and

Fewer anxiety and depressive symptoms.

Just as these benefits impact our day-to-day quality of life, the actions we take in support of our purpose are incremental and quotidian. Guru Rinpoche, the eighth-century Tibetan master who brought Buddhism from India to Tibet, once said that we should go through life "with our view as high as the sky and our actions as meticulous as finely ground *tsampa* [barley flour that is a staple in the Tibetan diet]." This is, to me, an important distinction to make about capital-*P* purpose. No matter how lofty our goal, we can't forget to keep our actions grounded. It's not about a moral crusade. It's about the everyday. Purpose encompasses our to-do list, our phone calls, our e-mails, our commutes. Applying purpose in this way is actually much sloppier than embarking on a moral crusade, and it is why it is a spiritual path that requires wisdom. Being sentimental or overly "capital *P*" in your purpose is not sustainable in the long run. It can undermine us because we can't live there 100 percent of the time. Life is more complicated than that.

Accomplish This: Define Your Purpose

Defining Your Purpose

Understanding what drives and motivates us enables us to invest in the things that help us live our purpose. When we are not certain what our purpose is, we can help define it by doing both a "top-down" and a "bottom-up" assessment. A top-down assessment is one in which you examine the big picture first. With a bottom-up assessment, then, you examine small, separate activities, observations, exchanges—in other words, the parts that make up the big picture.

Top-down Assessment:

- Make a list of your top five to ten values.
- Take inventory of your work and personal calendar. First, look at whether the way you spend your time offers an accurate expression of your values. For example, if giving is important to you, do you have time on your calendar to volunteer or give in other ways that are meaningful to you? Next, make a note next to each item on your calendar, indicating if each activity energizes or drains you. Finally, looking at your time holistically, note how much of it is spent on activities that are invigorating and how much is spent on things that are depleting.
- Examine what matters to you. If you've made note of values that apply only to a work context, expand your list to include your family, community, and spiritual belief system.

- Ask those whom you trust what they would say you care about or what brings you energy and excitement.
- Identify gaps between what makes you tick and your current actions. For example, are there values that you care about deeply that you don't spend any time enacting? What could you do differently to allocate more time or attention to the things that matter?

Bottom-up Assessment:

- Keep a journal for a period of time; perhaps start with one week. During that time, note which activities, observations, and exchanges drain you and which ones make you feel good.
- Set a calendar reminder to review your journal. When you do, look for patterns: can you identify insights or make generalizations about cause-effect relationships?
- Make a list of people you admire and mark down traits of theirs that you value. Ask yourself whether you embody any of these traits, and if not, think about why not.

After completing both the top-down and bottom-up assessments to identify your purpose, write down any revelations you've had. What has the exercise revealed? What gaps between your purpose and your actions do you want to address? You may also want to use your observations to inform your personal mission statement (see page 29).

Purpose Makes Us Healthier

Professor Steve Cole's research investigates the biological pathways by which social environments, including experience and behavior, influence gene expression by viral, cancer, and immune cell DNA. Cole is a profoundly practical person; he accomplishes more in a workweek than many of us would be proud to do in half a year. He has been a thought partner and adviser to me for a number of years now, as I've been trying to understand the research around purpose and apply it to the work I do with businesses, MBA students, parents, and veterans with post-traumatic stress disorder.

In the middle of September 2015, I went to visit Steve at UCLA. His office is in a funky 1970s-style building. After sharing the elevator ride up with a giant tank of something labeled "Biohazard," I wove my way through a labyrinth to his office, a small room with an enormous picture window overlooking the LA canyons. This, Steve tells me, is why he hasn't moved to the new building, a few blocks away. The lab is jammed floor to ceiling with expensive and serious-looking equipment. I promised not to touch anything as he toured me around and told me about his work.

One of Steve's favorite areas of gene expression research explores the biological impact of purpose. Call it "positive biology." After years spent studying genetic expression profile shifts associated with what kills us and how not to live, he decided to turn his attention to what we should be doing instead. Millennia-old questions about the nature of a good life and the true meaning of happiness are not only philosophical, Steve realized, but physiological. He went looking for answers directly by, as he puts it, "polling the opinion of the human genome."

For thousands of years, people have debated whether happiness is best pursued by seeking as many pleasurable experiences as possible (filling our time with things we enjoy doing and surrounding ourselves with people we like) or by pursuing meaning that is greater than we are. The former perspective is known as the hedonic approach. The second perspective (that genuine happiness is not derived from only short-term pleasant experiences, or "momentary euphoria") is the eudaimonic happiness that Aristotle, among others, endorsed. Steve took this age-old philosophical debate and made it a research question, to determine through the study of human genes which of these two approaches liberates us from a "molecular soup of death."

In one study, Steve and Dr. Barbara Fredrickson, a research psychologist at the University of North Carolina and a pioneer in the field of positive psychology, grouped a sample of eighty people according to their hedonic or eudaimonic approach to happiness. In addition to assessing depression and other psychometrics, the researchers drew blood from each participant and analyzed twenty-two thousand genes to see if a certain molecular profile correlated with either of these distinct ways of being in the world.[3]

In scientific terms, when it came to the participants' subjective self-reports of psychological measures, the outcomes across the two groups were not significantly different. A high level of hedonic well-being does function in our subjective experience, to keep us from feeling miserable or depressed. Objectively, however, as measured on a cellular level, the gene expression between the two groups was markedly different. Steve and his colleagues concluded that living with eudaimonic purpose comes with health benefits that hedonic happiness doesn't provide—specifically, less inflammation and more antivirals and antibodies, which are associated with decreased incidence of heart disease, cancer, and other chronic diseases. (This study has since been replicated, with similar findings.)

Everybody wants to be happy, but satisfying your emotional needs alone does not qualify as a capital-*P* purpose. And Steve's research suggests that failing to consider the needs of others in your pursuit of happiness can have an impact at the cellular level. Fulfillment that goes beyond self-gratification isn't just better for the world; it's better for our individual health.

Other studies offer compelling evidence that having a strong sense of purpose benefits our physical and mental health in numerous ways. Samuel Cohen at the University of Cambridge conducted a review[4] of ten studies involving 136,000 people and found that those with a diminished sense of purpose were "more likely to have a stroke, heart attack, or coronary artery disease requiring a stent or bypass surgery." Purposefulness is also associated with lower and more stable cortisol levels, lower waist-to-hip ratios, lower body weight, faster onset and longer duration of REM sleep, increased antibody response to flu vaccines, reduced emotional responses to negative stimuli, and lower risk of mortality, disability, and Alzheimer's disease.

Recognizing the impact of purpose across our lives, researchers are increasingly interested in assessing how having a sense of purpose in the workplace impacts our well-being. Alia Crum at Stanford and Ellen Langer at Harvard[5] are two psychologists investigating how our health is affected by our perspective on work. One of their studies involved eighty-four women with full-time jobs as room attendants in seven different hotels. The women were told they were participating in a study related to improving the health and happiness of hotel employees, and were then assigned to one of two groups. One group was told, before the researchers collected data, that their work cleaning hotel rooms was good exercise that more than satisfied the surgeon general's recommendations for an active lifestyle. The other group was given this information after the data were collected.

The behavior of the women in the "before" group didn't change over the four weeks of the study, but their physiological measures (including weight, body mass index, waist-to-hip ratio, and blood pressure) all showed significant improvement compared to those for the "after" group, which showed no improvement. The researchers came to the conclusion that simply thinking about your work in a more positive way can favorably impact your health.

As we've discussed, a toxic workplace is bad for your mental and physical health. But mindfulness, which helps you cultivate an awareness of your purpose, can mitigate some of those dangers. Purpose not only makes you more fulfilled; it also effectively detoxes the workplace.

Creating a Calling

The way we think about our daily tasks can change our relationship to our work. Thus, by changing our perspective, we can achieve a greater sense of purpose without actually changing what we're doing. Try the following:

1. Pick one upcoming task on your calendar, whether it be attending a meeting, giving a presentation, or filling out an expense report.

2. Think about the task, first, as part of a job, then as a career, and finally as a calling. Jot down or make mental notes for each of these different states.

3. Reflect on how you approach the task when you think of it as a duty for a job versus something you do as part of a calling. Does your motivation change? Do you feel a shift in excitement or, perhaps, more or less dread?

4. Practice doing this with a wider swath of your tasks. Take an entire day and reframe it as a calling. Pay attention to how a shift in your perspective impacts your sense of joy and purpose.

Purpose Helps You Overcome Obstacles

In addition to making our cells healthier and our jobs more satisfying, a sense of purpose can also help us overcome obstacles, a benefit that obviously makes a difference at work. Social psychologist Anthony Burrow[6] at Cornell University studies the utility of purpose and how it impacts behavior. His latest research looks at what motivates students to climb a steep hill in the middle of campus known as the Slope. He has conducted similar studies, using virtual slopes, to see if the mental calculations involved in climbing a hill are influenced by purpose in the virtual as well as the actual world. The goal of the experiment was to identify the correlation between a student's sense of purpose and the degree of difficulty with which he or she regarded the climb, to understand why some students make it up the Slope while others don't.

After climbing the hill, study participants were met at the top by a researcher who asked them to estimate the slope of the hill and the effort it took to climb it. Those participants who reflected on their larger purpose in life before climbing the hill estimated the slope of the hill and the effort to climb it as lower than if they had been asked to write about a short-term goal, something they wanted to accomplish that day. Those who had reflected on a neutral topic rather than either their life purpose or a short-term goal estimated the hill as steepest and the effort to climb it as highest. Students with a higher sense of purpose, therefore, while having no illusions about the size of the hill, perceived the effort differently, and the difficulty of the task did not inhibit their willingness to climb. Participants who experienced the effort as more significant also estimated the hill's slope as steeper.

What was groundbreaking in this study was that for people with either higher dispositional purpose (who perceived themselves as high in purpose) or who were asked to reflect on purpose only briefly, the link between effort and slope overestimation was diminished. They still saw the slope as challenging, but they were more accurate in sizing up the challenge than their less-purposeful colleagues, who overestimated the size of the slope.

It's not all that surprising that the students who didn't have a strong sense of purpose overestimated the size of the hill. The more interesting result, to me, is that a short-term goal didn't cut it, either. The most important factor in not overestimating the size of the hill was whether the students viewed the effort as part of a bigger-picture, longer-term journey.

If we apply these findings to the workplace, this might indicate that immediate, short-term goals may not be enough to motivate workers to correctly assess the size of a difficult task. The takeaway? If we want to understand what it is we are trying to do (a key part of actually being able to do it), we have to find ways to keep our greater purpose and vision in mind.

Purpose, Burrow believes, is wrapped up in the everyday things we do, the opportunities we take that further our goals, and the commitments we avoid because they don't help serve those goals. Through Burrow's work, the physical reality of the Slope has become a vivid metaphor for mental obstacles, in perfect correspondence with current thinking in psychology (not to mention thousands of years of Buddhist understanding) that suffering is not objective but is, rather, contingent upon how we frame our circumstances. Much of the time our stories about our experience are responsible for making our problems more difficult than they need to be. As Burrow puts it, "what we bring into the world affects our perception" of the world.[7]

This is not to suggest that suffering is relative in the sense that you are lucky if you have a job at all or are able to make a living wage. It is more about reframing what suffering is with your purpose in mind. If your suffering feels meaningless, well, you're probably not in the right job.

The clarity that purpose provides is part of its power. Purpose allows us to shift our perspective so that we can see larger meaning for our lives, which enables us to prioritize among conflicting drives, desires, and choices. It provides the motivation and willpower to implement our goals.

The notion of purpose as a guiding force in our lives has sometimes been criticized as a problem for the privileged few. Abraham
Maslow's hierarchy of needs,[8] a popular theory since the 1940s, suggests that meaning and "self-actualization" (as he referred to it) are
irrelevant until our other basic needs, such as food, clothing, shelter,
and safety, are met. The problem with theories like these is that while
there's no denying the importance of basic needs, life is more complex than checking off a series of boxes. In reality, examples abound of
people with a strong sense of purpose despite, or even because of, subpar socioeconomic circumstances: Holocaust survivors such as Misha
Kraus and Viktor Frankl; supporters of Mahatma Gandhi, Nelson
Mandela, Martin Luther King Jr.; and so on. The history of religion
can be seen as one massive example of less-well-off people seeking
meaning greater than themselves through community, nature, and
the divine (also of more-well-off people serving their own interests
and exploiting and oppressing others, of course, but the two are not
mutually exclusive). Given the positive relationship demonstrated by
Burrow and many others among purpose, motivation, and resilience,
a sense of purpose must be at least as important, if not more important, for people facing adversity such as poverty or war.

Research supports my impression. Kendall Cotton Bronk,[9] another leader in the field of purpose, found evidence of purposefulness among youth in Colorado who were formerly homeless and/or in
trouble with the law. Their purpose had its own sound, different from
the ideas of people with higher education and more money, but it was
no less moving: "To be an example because I come from a background
where people won't expect anything from me, and I want to prove
them wrong and show people that I can be like that," and "We can be
good people."

The health, satisfaction, and resilience benefits of purpose are significant for us individually, but purpose has interpersonal implications,
too, as we'll see in later chapters. Purpose makes us better coworkers

and, as Wrzesniewski's (and my) business students have discovered, better leaders. In our history as human beings, we have long recognized the power of purpose, and religion has been the place to get it. Today, as a culture of people who spend more hours at work than we do at home (and certainly more than we spend in places of worship), we can borrow techniques from contemplative traditions to bring purpose to the jobs we do.

Puzzling Your Purpose

Few work environments leverage the power of purpose more effectively than the military. Luke, one of my midcareer graduate students at Stanford and a lieutenant in the army, grew up in a family with many generations of military service. He told me about a metaphor that his father, Gen. Robert Van Antwerp, retired from the Army Corps of Engineers and now working as a leadership consultant, uses to convey the importance of purpose: a jigsaw puzzle.

A puzzle metaphor for life is not exactly unheard of, but Van Antwerp's emphasis on the box the puzzle comes in was a new angle for me. Luke grew up doing puzzles with his family, including his father the general and his brother, who is also an officer in the army. As the boys got older, their father would hide the box top and challenge his sons to do the puzzle without it. We need to keep our eye on the picture on the cover of the box, Luke says. We will spend a lot of time staring at the pieces, of course, and time trying to fit them this way or that, but it's the picture on the cover of the box that guides us. This is our bigger picture, the meaning of our life, our purpose. In order to complete the puzzle, we need to reference that box top more often than we might expect.

As with our purpose in life, so with our purpose in work—because they're the same thing. The Buddhist nun Pema Chödrön once wrote,

"There are no interruptions."[10] In other words, your life is your life, and all the pieces are part of the bigger picture. Getting pulled over on your way home from work, weeping in the break room because you had a bad fight with your partner the night before, experiencing the death of a pet when you're trying to meet a deadline, taking time off to have a baby, having to work on Christmas Day—it's all life. When we aspire to find a "work-life balance," we end up pitting one against the other: work interrupts life, or life interrupts work, but, either way, we feel resentful and screwed. From a different, more expansive perspective, there could be room for both.

We all share this need to see the bigger picture of our lives, and though our respective pictures may look different owing to our different circumstances, values, and experiences, the process of doing any jigsaw puzzle is fundamentally the same. Similarly, the methods tested by science (recently) and by wisdom traditions (for thousands of years) are useful no matter what your big picture looks like. Because work is such a big part of everyone's puzzle, it's important to consider how and where it fits into the puzzle box cover. It's important to ask yourself if your work is a part of that picture. Can you envision where the piece you're holding in your hand at the moment, or at any moment, fits into the bigger picture? In other, less metaphorical words, does it really matter whether you do this thing you're about to do? Ultimately, when you wake up in the morning, or on a Sunday night as you contemplate the workweek ahead, do you think it matters whether you show up for work? It should matter. The likelihood of it mattering greatly increases if you believe that what you do with your time on the job makes sense, that it's worth it.

As a mother of three young children, I ask myself weekly, if not daily, about missing so many moments with them. At nursery school drop-off, when my toddler is screaming and clinging to my leg, begging me not to leave, I need to feel that the trade-off is worth it—for me, for the world, for my family, for him. Underlying the debate about whether and how to "lean in" is the question of what my time away from my children feels like and how I make sense of it. Confidence in my decision to lean in, lean out, or sit up straight and proud comes more from my overall, puzzle-box-cover sense that whatever I'm doing is a piece, however small, of my big picture, of my purpose, than it does from how I divvy up the hours of my days. And it takes practice to be able to tap into that purpose in the moment, when my child is screaming, or later, as I flash back to it during the workday. This goes both ways: some Monday mornings, after particularly chaotic weekends, I savor the quiet at the office, the space to string together two thoughts in a row, and I feel slightly guilty that I am savoring it. Also, the quality of my time with my children, especially when they're not at their best, depends on my awareness that they're in the big picture, too.

"Worth it" depends on the person and on the day. For some of us, a clear financial upside to our work gives meaning to our days. For others, the meaning is in belonging: work relationships and culture are our reasons for getting out of bed. Perhaps one's meaning is found in participating in innovation, or serving people in need. For many if not most of us, it's a mix of things. Conversely, our purpose could be what's missing, if it has gotten hazy or was never clear. In any case, even those who've known the pleasure of deeply purposeful work can lose that loving feeling (with its attendant benefits) at some point along the way. Maybe we're burnt out from the acute stress of a demanding job or desensitized through the more diffuse stress of daily life in general. We may be so harried by routine tasks and demands, distracted by habits such as an addiction to electronic devices, our noses to our to-do lists, that we don't notice how we feel—or, conversely, we are so caught up in our feelings, whether good or bad, that we lose sight of the big picture. We may have strayed from our purpose gradually, one setback (or success) at a time. Maybe we're disillusioned from chafing against broken systems for too long, or we feel undervalued or unappreciated. Or we may feel off purpose in work but not in other parts of our lives, and with enough compartmentalization, we've stopped noticing the ache.

Yes, the opposite of "on purpose" is "off purpose," and that's how we feel when we do anything not on purpose—we feel off in one or more senses of the word, off course or shut down. It's understandable to cope with the discomfort and disappointment (or outright pain and horror) of being purposeless or off purpose by turning off altogether. We might bury ourselves in social media, binge-watch TV, eat or drink more than we'd like. No matter how lost or stuck or numb you feel, though, you're not helpless, you can get back on purpose. As with that jigsaw puzzle, start with the corner pieces.

Articulating Your Purpose

As I've mentioned, there are two approaches to articulating your purpose: top down and bottom up.

TOP-DOWN APPROACH

From the top down, we declare our purpose (or take a stab at it, at least) based on our conscious, espoused beliefs. We might start with a list of our top five values, for example, compassion, authenticity, etc. Studies have shown that articulating our core values amplifies our resilience and makes us feel less depleted after efforts that require willpower, such as staying on task or saying no to a donut. Once you've articulated your values, ask yourself whether those values include your own well-being, the well-being of the people close to you (at home or at work), your local community, the world.

These questions may heighten your awareness of discrepancies between your stated values and how you actually spend your time. This is perfectly normal. It is not cause for alarm or self-flagellation but, rather, a prime opportunity to see the gaps and make choices about how to respond. That's what this book is all about. I also encourage you to reflect on conversations with people who know you well and whom you trust. Ask them what they notice about what you appear to value (one of the questions I have my students ask in a survey they send out to their friends and colleagues is what you do when you are at your best), and see if they add to your thought process. In my class, I have my students send out questionnaires to friends, colleagues, and family asking what they have observed about when they (the students) are most passionate or purposeful. I have done this exercise myself. And more informally, I enlist the counsel of my own personal board of directors of mentors and colleagues.*

Purpose can emerge in more than one way. Most experts promote either the top-down approach (as in the exercise I've just described) or the bottom-up approach (as in the exercises to follow), but not both. I recommend going at it from both directions, in a spirit of experimentation. From the bottom up, we excavate rather than declare. We let the picture emerge from indirect questions and nonverbal exercises. Often, our core beliefs are invisible to us, unrecognized by our conscious mind. This makes them hard to articulate with rational concepts and literal language. Bottom-up approaches tap into our emotional and embodied experience as well as our logic, recognizing that somewhere, buried under current routines and circumstances, we have a sense about what matters to us that is more or less accessible. The bottom-up approach digs through to find the part of us that knows what we are about. The top-down approach helps us map the larger interests in our lives and jobs to the tasks we need to get done on any given day.

---

* Take a look at this list of purpose training techniques: www.leahweissphd.com /purposetrainingtechniques.

Instead of asking, "What is my purpose?" and trying to answer directly, you might prefer one of these bottom-up approaches. Be patient with yourself. Bottom-up approaches may require some time and meandering before you get the answers you're looking for.

» **Track Your Sense of Purpose**

Pick a manageable period of time, such as one week, to pay attention as you go about your business, and notice when you feel most on purpose and what you're doing at the time. Note these associations in a journal or document you keep for this . . . yes, purpose. What does purpose feel like? you might well ask. It can be a feeling of vitality, when making an effort leaves us energized rather than drained. One of my graduate students noticed that she was "on the edge of her seat" at a lecture and realized that it spoke to what she cared about most. Purpose can also feel calm, because when what we're doing on the ground lines up with our higher purpose (when a puzzle piece fits), our inner critics have less to talk about; we stop second-guessing what we're doing and just do it. There's a peaceful feeling of relief. We may notice an attendant sense of pride—or Mihaly Csikszentmihalyi's famous "flow,"[11] when we're so absorbed in what we're doing that it feels effortless and we're oblivious to time passing. People describe it as a feeling of being alive. When do you feel, or have you felt, most alive?

At the end of the week, or however long you keep track, review your notes. Do you see any pattern to your sense of purpose? Does it tend to come with certain categories of things you do? Can you make any generalizations about your purpose from the specific instances of it during this time?

If you need more time for patterns to emerge, you can try this zoomed-out visual version of tracking in the form of a "lifeline." Draw the ups and downs of your life in a line, charting "peak" and "valley" experiences, and look for patterns and themes among them to reveal what motivates you and what matters. What got you from this valley to that peak? Your lifeline can be more or less detailed and inclusive, covering many areas or focusing on just one, and spanning any number of years (adolescence, for example), so long as it's enough to include both peaks and valleys—enough data for patterns to emerge. (In any case, this exercise comes with a built-in, perspective-enhancing assumption: peaks and valleys are natural, and all human lives have them.)

» **Visualize Your Purpose**

In Stanford's Compassion Cultivation Training, we sometimes do a visualization in the first week to help participants surface their purpose for taking the course: Try imagining yourself in a field with a well. Pick up a stone embedded with a question about your intentions for something you do (work or otherwise). Picture throwing the stone into a well and see what answers come up from inside of you—they may not be whole answers, but many people have been surprised by the telling words and images that would not have occurred to them if they'd been asked directly.

» **Mirror Your Purpose**

Alternatively, think of people you admire and trace what you like about them back to your own values. Tenzin Priyadarshi, of the Dalai Lama Center for Ethics at MIT, draws on aspirational figures in his transformational leadership trainings. Reflecting on the inspirational qualities of a Desmond Tutu or a Ruth Bader Ginsburg or a Beyoncé will shine a light on ourselves. In the traditional Buddhist metaphor, the person we look up to functions as a mirror for our own best self. Closer to home, you may appreciate someone you work with. What is it about this person? Aspirational figures don't have to be perfect any more than you do: an ability to gracefully navigate ordinary departmental snafus may suffice. Just focus on the qualities you admire. (If you can't think of anyone you admire at work, that in itself might tell you something.)

My business school students do these top-down and bottom-up exercises at home and then share in class what they've learned. To give you an idea of how this process plays out in real life, here are a few examples from their experiences:

My biggest revelation was the valley [when I drew my lifeline]. The points in my life in which I've felt I'm distinctly wandering from my purpose are those in which I've had to obscure my motivations or otherwise relevant information from those I'm working with or that depend on me. Which led me to think about my values of transparency and honesty. As part of my purpose in life, I intend to be as transparent and honest as I can, especially with those people with whom I share a common goal or objective. I think I worked toward that purpose this week, but there was in fact very little opportunity to practice it.

I found that I don't spend much of my time with my purpose at the forefront. I do prioritize my children, but I also feel pulled to chase things that don't matter to me. This week I attended a talk on diversity in academia. I love the research on gender diversity, and these discussions directly relate to what I'm passionate about, but I almost didn't attend in order to get my classwork done. Fortunately, I did attend and found myself at the edge of my seat for most of the talk. How do I find a way to pursue this purpose with additional intention and determination?

I don't know what my purpose is. In fact, I failed miserably at the in-class exercise and had zero recollection of feelings during *my life highs and lows. But, as the dung beetle* suggested, if I approach purpose from values, I may be able to get close. I value empathy above all else. I melt when I see an act of thoughtful kindness, and I boil when I see a selfish disregard of others.*

If the picture you have of your purpose is nonexistent or really unclear, give yourself time to experiment with the exercises in this section, read graphic novels, sleep on it, and don't panic if a clear vision doesn't immediately present itself. Getting to know your purpose is, in itself, an entirely respectable purpose. Purpose is ongoing and iterative. It's a process of seeing what works and what doesn't. You can always revise your purpose.

How to Get Unstuck

When we feel "stuck" creatively, we may be constricted by our own narrow perspective. We're stuck in ourselves. The traditional Buddhist antidote to this is an "offering practice," which entails visualizing giving away possessions, credit, or social status to a symbol of awakening or freedom. In other, more practical terms, if I'm stuck in my writing, I recall my purpose in writing (helping people, fulfilling my longing to communicate) and then offer the challenge to this greater purpose. I can do this in my head, or write about it for three minutes, or the offering can take a symbolic, physical form, as in lighting a candle (if I'm working from home) or putting a meaningful object in front of an image that represents my highest purpose. You could put an image in your work space

---

* The "dung beetle" refers to something in a graphic novel by Vic Strecher that I assign to my students. It's called *On Purpose*, and I recommend it to you, too.

that stands for your highest goals for your work and leave a piece of fruit or chocolate in front of it. At some point later in the day, you could offer that sweet to a coworker, put it in the break room for someone to find as a surprise, or enjoy it mindfully yourself.

» **Amplify Your Purpose**

It may be fine and good that we have a sense of our puzzle box cover, but given the complexity of our lives, how do we go beyond identifying our purpose and cultivating it in our everyday lives, especially at work? The answer lies in taking what we know about mindfulness and putting it into action. By making consistent efforts to clarify our intentions and align our attention and action with our purpose, even during mundane tasks, we can keep a sense of purpose at the forefront of our lives.

Putting purpose into action doesn't require grand gestures. You don't need to take refugees into your home. You don't need to quit your job and move to an ashram. But because a higher purpose is meant to be high, a big picture bigger than each of us alone, having and expressing a purpose is by nature a daunting, potentially dizzying task that may leave us feeling more "Now what?" than inspired. We think we can't reach that high, and we don't know how to bring our purpose down to earth.

A higher purpose first meets real life in our intentions. We tend to underestimate the power of intentions to affect our actions when, in fact, intentions are the first critical step to living our purpose. We can't begin to close the gap between how things are and how we mean them to be if we don't know how we mean them to be. The truth is, if we want our behavior to bear some resemblance to our intentions (and by the definition of "intention," we can assume we do), it's not enough to set them once and forget about them. We have to remember them. We have to remember to remember, and then we have to re-remember, to look up every now and then. We remind ourselves by consciously, repeatedly setting our intention.

In traditional Buddhist intention-setting practice, we say things like "May I be a protector for those who are without protectors, a guide for travelers, and a boat, a bridge, and a ship for those who wish to cross over. May I be a lamp for those who seek light, a bed for those who seek rest, and may I be a servant for all beings who desire a servant. To all sentient beings may I be a wish-fulfilling gem, a vase of good fortune, an efficacious mantra, a great medication, a wish-fulfilling tree, and a wish-granting cow." Imagine if, instead of "I hate Mondays" or some such, *that* was your first thought of the day. Mahayana Buddhist practitioners cultivate an "awakened mind" (*bodhicitta*); they awake to wisdom and compassion by, among other things, reciting lines that articulate high transpersonal goals of awakening and happiness for the benefit of all beings and that affirm the practitioner's intention to become an instrument of these ideals. In Abrahamic traditions, people pray to become an agent of God's will.

In a secular practice, our intentions may sound simpler, and we might play it a little cooler, but they're no less powerful. With whatever words make sense and feel right to us (language we arrived at through the previous top-down or bottom-up exercises, for example), we set our best intentions for doing something before we do it. "Something" could be a day, for which we set our intentions each morning. ("Today, I intend to give people my full attention when they're talking to me, because I want to live in a world where we haven't forgotten how to do that.") It could be a phone call from a friend. ("I don't have much time and that can come across as impatience. The main thing is that I let him know how much I value his friendship.") We can think our intention or say it out loud, and as we practice doing so, we might find we need fewer or even no words. "Today, really listen" could become our shorthand in the morning—and we would know what that meant. Or, as we all get a feeling when we think about what a particular friendship means to us, we could invoke this felt sense of our intention in a moment, in the time it takes our friend to greet us. We feel it in our heart. We take the extra minute in the break room to ask a colleague about her grandchild, and we listen to her update.

The more we practice setting an intention, the readier access we'll have to the sense of purpose in that intention. The more often we remember an intention, the more quickly we'll notice when our behavior is off. This is how we imbue moments and days with meaning. We can practice with meetings, phone calls, commutes, helping our kids get dressed in the morning, and the last thing we say to our partner at night. There's nothing we can't practice with, in fact. Everything counts.

In traditional societies, religious rituals and community customs served as reminders of one's purpose. You don't forget to go to church or temple when "everyone" is doing it and "everyone" is expecting you to do it, too. In modern, individualistic, secular society, we fend for ourselves, without this structural support and with a whole lot more to distract us from our purpose. We don't inherit a common purpose with communal habits to remind us, so we must forge them ourselves.

Radical Prioritization

Having a clear purpose isn't a one-and-done thing. Yes, we first need to work to articulate our purpose, and this helps us set our direction, but then we need to revisit our purpose over and over and over. Having a North Star doesn't help if we don't look up at it. We often ask ourselves how we can best align our behavior to our purpose. Each time we glance at our to-do list is an opportunity to enact our purpose, a chance to remind ourselves that we can bring our actions into alignment with our intentions. Living with intention requires that we continually and consciously place our attention on the things that support our purpose, and one of the key ways we do this is to prioritize.

Prioritization—the clarity about what to do and what not to do, and the recognition that the many things that are possible to do can be a great distraction from the thing that most needs doing—happens to be a skill that both great spiritual practitioners and effective business leaders have in common. The first of the practices you would do in the context of traditional Buddhist prioritization would be to reflect on mortality. The point of our remembering that life is short is not to depress ourselves or be a buzz kill to others. It is to help us put things in perspective, to prioritize what matters most, and to cultivate the willingness to do that without delay.* Prioritization does not require perfection, but it does require revisiting again and again. The *dampa sum* process ("good in the beginning, good in the middle, good in the end") is on point with this approach: setting intentions, doing something in line with those intentions, revisiting how it went, reflecting and resetting intentions, and then changing plans as needed.

Buddhism does not have a monopoly on practices that bring our attention to our purpose throughout the day, week, year. The millennia-old insight that Franciscans bring into their daily cycle of prayer, meal, study, prayer, and service is another example of ritualized intention. It was a Franciscan priest in Jamaica Plain, Massachusetts, Father Jack Rathschmidt, who first introduced me to the futility of trying to balance everything. I was in grad school at the time, pregnant, facing the wrath of my committee not only for interrupting my studies to have a baby but also for planning to move across the country. Father Jack pointed out that the metaphor of balance keeps us holding everything. He said that a better way to manage multiple tasks is to think about maintaining a rhythm. Rhythm lets us do the one thing that matters most while we move through our days and weeks, tending to other obligations as we go.

---

* Learn more about Buddhist prioritization methods here: www.leahweissphd.com /buddhistprioritization.

Radical prioritization means recognizing that we are never going to solve the problem of having too much to do by shrinking the amount we have to do. We can't change our workload, we can't downgrade our responsibilities, but we can change how we think about what we have to do and how we engage with the process of prioritizing.

Keep Your Eyes on the Prize

Choosing what to pay attention to and envisioning how you would like it to go is a fundamental act of creativity. The reality is, whether we realize it or not, we construct our world all the time. With mindfulness, we bring intentionality to the process, instead of accidentally finding ourselves in worlds we didn't know we were making and that we'd rather not be in. Buddhist and other religious practices have harnessed the power of visualization for millennia. More recently, contemporary psychology has picked up on it in performance contexts such as professional sports and work. As sociologist and O magazine columnist Martha Beck has written, "It's not so much that if we picture something happening, it certainly will happen (it's not magic) as that if we can't picture something happening, it probably won't. Envision the outcome you want."

When we are juggling multiple priorities, it often feels as if they were in conflict with one another and are pulling us in many directions. In this situation, the setting of priorities can get confusing. How do we keep alive the sense of what matters? And if we're losing track with the big things, through the minutiae of our days, is it even possible to stay oriented to our purpose?

That's the goal of the workplace huddle, an increasingly common practice across business sectors. For many of us, what actually needs to happen in any given day does not always align with what's on our calendar. The huddle starts the day by helping us set an agenda (or intention) of the most important thing to focus on for the day. If a huddle doesn't seem like a realistic practice to integrate into your workplace, you can replicate this idea by having a morning huddle in your head. Identify the most important task on your to-do list and prioritize as needed to support your ability to attend to it.

There is a growing school of thought that to-do lists are useless, that they dull us to our real priorities. I had a student who lost her to-do list—she kept it in an old-school paper journal, not on a device—and reported that after the initial panic had subsided, she felt liberated. And she realized that most of what was on that list were silly items she was spending time shifting around or putting off from one week to the next.

Within the context of our work, the fear that we won't be able to do it all, the fear that paralyzes us from doing anything, can be mediated if we come back to the question of what matters most, right now, in this moment—that is, what is our priority. We can ask ourselves and/or our teams: What need must be met, what problem most needs to be solved? That is what should be tended to, not the thing we slotted into our quarterly plan for today. And because (lucky us) we have been practicing the skill of intentionally directing our attention, we can recognize when we have gone down a rabbit hole of another task or on an all-out diversion.

Fridays are a good time to check in with your internal project manager. How well were you able to bring your attention to each task? Did you execute the plan you laid out for the week, bringing a sense of purpose to each activity? Remember, though: your road map isn't meant to be written in stone. In fact, planning and honing your attention should equip you with the confidence to jettison a plan, say no, cancel, or delegate if necessary, so that you can consistently focus your time where it will best serve your end goals. And you can begin the new week by touching base with your highest purpose.

It's all too easy to allow entire days to pass by in a blur without articulating what you've actually done. Instead, realize that your days are made up of thousands of discrete moments passing before you, and that you can consciously choose to make the most of them. Knowing what you are doing and why allows you not only to feel accomplishment in doing your work well, but also to have a more fulfilling sense that your days actually matter.

Mindful purpose allows us to conjure the possibility of our best selves, our best work, and our best lives. It helps us reorient ourselves when we become lost and inspires us when we become stuck. And when we approach each day with intention, we ensure that the light of this faraway star can continue to guide us. In practice in our real lives, at our actual workplaces, living in accordance with our purpose might mean something as simple as effectively prioritizing the tasks and to-dos that pave the way to our larger goals. Some days we win big; other days, small. Either way, though, it matters to us, to the people around us, to our organizations, and ultimately to the world whether we show up with purpose.

Part II

———————

BRINGING OUR WHOLE "SELVES" TO THE OFFICE

4

Cultivating Compassion

THERE ARE TWO GREAT FORCES OF HUMAN NATURE: SELF-INTEREST, AND
CARING FOR OTHERS, AND PEOPLE ARE SUCCESSFUL WHEN THEY ARE
DRIVEN BY A "HYBRID ENGINE" OF THE TWO.

Bill Gates, at the World Economic Forum, 2008

Several years ago, a heartwarming story received a lot of coverage in the press. It focused on an elderly woman named Edith Macefield, who lived in a little house in Seattle. Development in her neighborhood was booming, with new condos and apartment buildings replacing old single-family homes. Real estate developers wanted to build a mall on Edith's street and offered her $750,000 for her little house and property, which was worth about $120,000. When she turned down the offer, the developers increased the number to $1 million, which she also turned down. So they decided to build the mall around her home. Soon after the construction began, it surrounded her house on three sides. The superintendent of the project, Barry Martin, would occasionally drop by Edith's house to make sure she was okay. He gave her his business card, telling her to call him if she needed anything.

One day, she took Barry up on that offer and asked if he could drive her to a hair appointment. He obliged, and over time, he began to take her to all her appointments. As they got to know each other, she shared her life history with him. She had some amazing stories that seemed hard to believe—such as the one about being a spy during World War II or being cousins with Benny Goodman. Though he was skeptical at first, Barry eventually found evidence that Edith's larger-than-life tales were all true. As time went on, he eventually became her primary caregiver.

By the time Edith died of pancreatic cancer at age eighty-six, Barry was scheduling her doctor's appointments, preparing her meals, and visiting her whenever he could. Despite the conflict with his role at work, the age difference, and Edith's need for so much intensive time and care, he had come to care deeply for her, and he was the one who was there for her at the end.

Barry and Edith's unlikely friendship made for easy press fodder because it was a classic David-and-Goliath scenario come to life: the aggressive real estate developer and the helpless old lady, both of whom end up being much more than they appear at first glance. But what I love most about this story is that, somehow, despite their not-insignificant conflict, Edith and Barry managed to do a miraculous thing. They saw each other as human first, and as a result of their recognizing their shared humanity, a caring relationship formed that was meaningful to the both of them.

This kind of event, this breaking through of barriers to relate to a person, a person who may be on the opposite side of an issue important to you, requires a skill that is an essential component of mindfulness: compassion. When, like Barry and Edith, we are able to view others as part of the human condition, as imperfect, bumbling works in progress (just like us!), when we resist the impulse to "other" them or reduce them to one dimension, we adapt the perspective necessary to develop compassion.

What Is Compassion?

Compassion as a concept is, I've been told, overexposed, yet I still think it is widely misunderstood. Like many principles of mindfulness, compassion is both simple and complex. The definition of compassion is fairly straightforward: being able and willing to recognize suffering and choosing to lean into it rather than avoid it. Acting with compassion can be a little trickier. Compassion might take the form of lending a hand to an overwhelmed coworker. Or it might involve telling a teammate that her communication style is negatively impacting the people around her. Compassion is respecting someone enough to call him out on his BS and encouraging him to be stronger and more accountable. Compassion doesn't mean avoiding difficult or uncomfortable conversations, but facing them head-on.

In the Cultivating Compassion Training I helped develop alongside Thupten Jinpa, the Dalai Lama's principal interpreter for thirty years, we define compassion as a recognition of suffering, a feeling of concern and connection, a desire to relieve suffering, and a willingness to act as a result. Compassion is not about pitying another person's distress, being a hero, always saying yes, being naïve, or allowing yourself to become a doormat. As Jinpa says, "Compassion cultivation practice does not entail blurring the distinction between one's friends and foes; rather, it teaches a method whereby the fact that someone is a stranger or a foe does not automatically preclude the possibility of caring about his or her pain and sorrow."

There is a practice in Buddhism of seeing one's adversary as a spiritual teacher. But Buddhism hasn't cornered the market on the idea of treating others with dignity and respect. Christianity, Judaism, and Islam all have strong articulations of compassion not only to those with whom we are close but also, importantly, to strangers and the people we struggle against. Most contemplative traditions advocate the possibility of extending love and compassion even to one's adversaries. Christianity's reluctance to cast the first stone is based in the concept of our shared imperfection. In the Jewish synagogue, God is referred to as "the compassionate one," and Jews are called upon to "love [the stranger] as yourself." In the Qur'an, "whatever God grants his messenger in booty from the people of the towns belongs to God and his Messenger, as also to kinsmen, the orphans, the poor and the needy wayfarer, in order that wealth does not circulate solely among those of you who are rich." The world's contemplative traditions envision the human heart as capable of reaching such heights of feeling that, instead of responding to harm with hostility and vengefulness, one responds to the perpetrator with compassion and understanding.

While we can learn a lot about compassion from the wisdom traditions, compassion isn't and shouldn't be limited to the confines of places of worship. It is a universal value, one that must be implemented in supermarket lines and rush-hour traffic, in schools and workplaces, anywhere where too many of us are hurting.

According to a study conducted by Accountemps and reported in *Fortune*, managers and executives at Fortune 1000 firms spend 13 percent of their work time (the equivalent of seven weeks a year) mending employee relationships and otherwise dealing with the aftermath of incivility. Incivility is defined as rudeness at work, and is the research area of Georgetown professor Christine Porath.[1] What she and other researchers have found is that incivility costs companies a huge amount. Porath's most recent paper on the topic cites a "Civility in America" poll that shows that 70 percent of Americans "believe that incivility has reached crisis proportions."[2]

The reality is that people would rather blow up projects than see someone they hate succeed at them, or pay a consultant because they don't want a colleague they don't like to solve a problem and get the credit. Researchers have studied the bottom-line cost of professional relationships gone sour. When people are in an uncivil work environment, half will intentionally work less efficiently, half will have more sick days, a third will decrease the quality of their work intentionally, 80 percent will waste time worrying about an uncivil relationship, 60 percent will spend time avoiding another person, 78 percent said their commitment to the organization declined, and 25 percent admitted they took their hostility out on customers. Plus, people in an uncivil work environment make more mistakes—which Porath attributes to the brain (specifically the working memory) being "hijacked" by processing the rudeness. Creativity also goes down when people witness rudeness in the workplace. And this rudeness isn't rare behavior; it's on the rise. Nearly half of those surveyed in 1998 reported that they were treated rudely at least once a month, a figure that rose to 55 percent in 2011 and 62 percent in 2016. And this leads to a huge expense in terms of employee turnover.

Incivility is one thing—most of us have, at some point, experienced an unpleasant interpersonal dynamic at work—but it can be a real problem when it turns into bullying. The job search engine CareerBuilder[3] recently surveyed more than 5,600 people about their experience of workplace rudeness. More than 25 percent of people who responded said they experience bullying in the workplace. And this is not an anomaly—the American Psychological Association[4] has estimated that bullying and other types of abusive behavior at work cost businesses $300 billion annually in lost productivity, absenteeism, turnover, and increased medical costs. People who feel bullied aren't focusing on doing their jobs; they are focused on their unhappiness, talking to others about their unhappiness, and searching for another job.

One way to mitigate some of this unhappiness at work, for ourselves and others, is to mindfully practice compassion. I like to think of compassion as a cultivation, as something we ritualize into our day.

Compassion is something we do, not just something we feel. Compassion is found in our moment-by-moment choice not to roll our eyes at someone or gossip about her but, rather, to be with the awkward feeling we experience in response to her behavior—and to know that sometimes we, too, can evoke that feeling in others.

Ultimately, compassion is often best defined as an awareness of our imperfections that lends us the ability to be patient with other people's imperfections. This key insight comes out of mindfulness practice and leads to expressing compassion from the perspective of an equal with others. It is not looking down on others whose suffering is greater than ours or looking up at the Dalai Lama with the belief that he is more capable than we are. We are all human, all capable of feeling and acting with compassion.

There is mounting evidence that practicing compassion in the workplace offers real results. For starters, compassion makes us more effective, healthier, and more resilient. It helps us learn, innovate, provide better service, cooperate, collaborate, be candid, avoid burnout, deal with "difficult" people, and acquire and retain talent.

But perhaps most important, compassion connects us with other people—and the power of human connection at work cannot be understated. Work is one of the ways in which we belong in the world, and the meaning of our work derives in large part from its use or value to others. For example, people who have more friends at work meet more deadlines than those with fewer friends, because they care more about how their work affects others and feel more responsible to the team. Feeling connected to our colleagues also allows us to draw out their ideas, which helps in strategic collaborations. While many corporate cultures encourage competition, it's important to draw the line between stimulating workers to engage and creating a toxic environment that gets in the way of their productivity. When we approach our coworkers as competitors, all our work suffers.

Compassion Is Good for Your Health

Compassion provides the ability for us to have stronger and more enjoyable relationships, and research shows that social connection is crucial to our health and well-being. Across 148 separate studies (with a total of 308,849 participants), a lack of social connection was found to be a greater detriment to health than obesity, smoking, or high blood pressure.[5] This finding remained consistent across age, sex, initial health status, cause of death, and follow-up period. Conversely, strong social connections strengthen our immune system, decrease inflammation at the cellular level, and help us recover from disease faster. The quality of our relationships may even lengthen our life—strong social connections have been linked to a 50 percent increase in longevity.

Remember, despite our tending to think of personal sacrifice as necessary for professional success, one's well-being and workplace success are relational, and this relationship ultimately boils down to our ability to connect meaningfully with others. In this way, compassion benefits our whole lives.

It is true, of course, that some degree of competition is natural and even advantageous. But lest you dismiss my championing of a compassionate workplace as hopelessly naïve, consider this: Evolution doesn't select only for competition and aggression. Though Charles Darwin's name is synonymous with the phrase "survival of the fittest," Darwin also said that "those communities which included the greatest number of the most sympathetic members would flourish best, and rear the greatest number of offspring."[6] In keeping with the lexicon of his day, Darwin refers to this quality as "sympathy," but what he was really talking about was compassion. From the perspective of evolutionary biology, compassion is a prosocial, cooperative instinct that helps to keep groups together, enhances care for vulnerable offspring and group members, supports social credit and group survival, and allows for cooperative relations with those outside one's "tribe."

Genetically speaking, we share more DNA with our fellow humans as compared to other species, even our closest ape cousins. Evolutionarily speaking, we come from the same "hundred mothers" as traceable through mitochondrial DNA. So there is actually a scientific basis for thinking that others are "just like me" or even that "everyone is my mother." This idea of our common humanity (or, as I like to think of it, our shared quandary) is predicated on the notion that other people are suffering and that their suffering is like our own. From this perspective, compassion becomes possible.

This psychological construct of tapping into our shared experience isn't about comparing or minimizing suffering—everyone has problems, and big or small, those problems are all real. The idea that you don't have the right to be anxious about a high-stakes presentation when there are homeless and hungry people in the world isn't helpful to anyone. So, when daily stressors threaten to get the better of us, the perspective of shared humanity can be helpful. It is reassuring to know that you aren't alone in your suffering; that we all have a shared history, a shared origin, this shared quandary. Chances are, for example, other people in your meeting are nervous about their role in a presentation. The people sitting in the conference room may be feeling any variety of difficult emotions about something that happened in their day. When we identify our commonality with others, we are able to highlight our similarities rather than our differences.

The writer Susan Sontag once said, "Serious fiction writers think about moral problems practically. They tell stories. They narrate. They evoke our common humanity in narratives with which we can identify, even though the lives may be remote from our own. They stimulate our imagination. The stories they tell enlarge and complicate—and, therefore, improve—our sympathies. They educate our capacity for moral judgment." I found this quote in her *Los Angeles Times* obituary, and it struck me as a perfect articulation of how to practice compassion. When we look at the world through the prism of a shared humanity, we free ourselves from our own boring perspective. When we can try on another person's worldview, we develop a greater capacity for ethical behavior, and that includes in the workplace.[*]

This doesn't mean that when someone screws up, we smile and ignore his mistake or let him off the hook easily. Rather, instead of flying off the handle or assuming the worst, we might start by finding out what he was thinking or what happened in his day or week that might have precipitated his screw-up. Second, recognize that we might be angry or frustrated by the impact of his behavior but that we will get to a better resolution and plan for moving forward if we take in his side of the story and then make a plan that prevents a similar mistake from happening again.

It also helps us be less judge-y. Judging sucks, for everyone. For the judge (because it is alienating and sour) as well as for the people being judged. It is a bad habit that practice can change. Instead of judging, we can try to be curious. Instead of doubling down on our initial idea about a person or situation, we can pause and ask ourselves if our interpretation is accurate. Maybe we think a person is being standoffish to us but in actuality they are exhausted from caring for a sick child the night before, and their behavior has nothing to do with us. Or maybe our interpretation is incomplete. Maybe we are correct in thinking he acted rudely to us, but what is going on in his life that has him behaving this way? What might we be missing about the situation? What role did we play in the difficult encounter; what was our contribution? This might seem like a drain to actually do—who has time for all of these inquiries and countersuppositions? Yet thinking

---

[*] Here are some more ways to cultivate the common humanity mind-set: www.leah weissphd.com/commonhumanitymindset.

about what might be influencing another person's behavior, let alone caring about what might be causing their suffering, may sound unpleasant, but in fact, it can make us feel good, too.

Brian Knutson[7] is a professor of psychology and neuroscience at Stanford. His research focuses on the experience and expression of emotion. Knutson uses fMRI technology to gain a deeper understanding of how emotion shows up in the brain and how it impacts our behavior. He's particularly interested in the nucleus accumbens region of the brain, which receives a hit of the feel-good neurotransmitter dopamine when a person anticipates a pleasurable experience.

In one study, Knutson set out to discover whether this feel-good response was activated by altruistic experience in the same way we know it is triggered by hedonistic experience. Recruiting Tibetan monastics, who are advanced in their ability to generate compassion at will, he asked them to practice compassion meditation in the fMRI machine. Knutson found that the experience of generating compassion toward suffering activated the same reward regions in the monks' brains that light up when the rest of us, motivated by hedonistic rewards, think about a donut or anticipate a vacation. (Sure, it is bizarre that in order to make this point, we needed to put monastics in an fMRI machine, but honestly, if the monks and nuns are up for it and what we learn is that caring for others is a win-win, I'm not going to worry too much about it.)

The work Brian Knutson is doing is vital, because it turns the idea of compassion on its head. It shows us not only that can we practice and become more agile in extending compassion, but also that compassion doesn't require our being miserable ourselves. If we could get that idea out—that this compassion business is actually the key to a good (and healthy) life—it would make a tremendous difference in our reallocating our time and attention toward service to others.

Some people worry that if we practice compassion to feel better or to be healthier ourselves, it undermines the whole point of being less self-absorbed. Is it actually compassion if it is self-referential? I've found, based on what I've seen in thousands of people, that our perspective on what compassion is and how it works changes when we start to make it a practice rather than when we see it as a philosophical principle or something we mull over at a distance. In other words, sure, maybe we practice compassion because we feel lonely and want stronger social connections. And when we start paying more attention to the struggles of others, we feel differently about not just them but ourselves. We see ourselves differently. We interact differently. And that's okay.

Compassion doesn't have to mean being a *Monty Python*–esque caricature of a self-flagellating spiritual figure. Most people who inspire us, who have spiritual wisdom, aren't depressed or miserable. They are out of their own way enough to make a real impact on the world. In fact, beating up on ourselves and feeling we need to feel bad is itself a form of self-preoccupation. In Buddhism, we practice giving, first, from one hand to the other, and then to people we are close to—and, bit by bit, our generosity improves.

Some practitioners of compassion resent the current-day practice of "measuring" compassion using scientific methods. Matthew Sacchet, a doctoral student in neuroscience at Stanford working with Knutson, offered his take on the controversy: "There's a concern that scientists might be 'trying to prove meditation,' but we are scientists trying to understand the brain," he said. "The research has important possibilities for medicine, and it could also get rid of some of the fuzz and help make meditation more empirically grounded." I agree with Sacchet that this research is a game changer: if compassion were seen as something we did not only because it was the right thing to do but also because it felt good, we might be more likely to do it.

The findings of this study are consistent with findings from similar research Knutson is doing in neuroeconomics that shows that financial rewards are less motivating than rewards related to intrinsic motivation (our sense of purpose), purpose (caring about the shared goal), and connection (being part of a team). This information is potentially useful if we are interested in motivating ourselves and others at work. We need to keep in mind that purely financial incentives aren't going to be the best motivator. If we can tie performance goals to the big-picture purpose that motivates coworkers, then the impact will be significantly amplified. When you are overcoming the challenges of, say, a product launch, shipping a product on time in return for a bonus is a goal. Shipping a product you believe is going to improve the lives of the recipients, even in some small way, will be much more motivating.

All these studies offer great evidence of the usefulness of compassion at work. The key question is how to get from here to there—from our seemingly automatic responses of judgment, anger, annoyance, or pity to compassion and connection. It isn't by holding ourselves to unrealistic standards or by feeling guilty for not being a "better person." It is by systematically training ourselves to develop an awareness of our negative default responses to the people who challenge us and choosing to respond in a different way, a way that honors their dignity, a way that allows them to be complicated, that assumes they are doing their best, and that understands that they are imperfect, just like the people we care about. Just like us.

We don't have to create or construct this truth. We just need something to snap us back to reality when we forget it.

Accomplish This:
Practicing Compassion Toward Others

Almost all of us can name one person (a boss, coworker, the person who sends a million e-mails) who drives us crazy at work. While it may seem impossible to feel anything but annoyance toward this individual, especially when she is creating more work for us or is the perceived cause of our suffering, by practicing compassion we can start to positively impact our work environment and change our experience. Try the following exercise to cultivate compassion:

- Bring the difficult person to mind.
- Imagine her outside of work—perhaps interacting with her children or taking a walk in nature.
- Imagine possible insecurities or life disappointments that led to the behaviors you find bothersome.
- Imagine separating the person from those things that cause the undesirable behavior.
- Think of people in this individual's life who care about and value her: a family member who relies on her or struggling parents who did their best to raise her.
- What behaviors does she display that you can appreciate: humor, the ability to get things done?
- Think of crossing paths with this person outside your normal environment—can you imagine meeting her for the first time and enjoying her company?

With this additional context for the person you find challenging, notice how it allows you to exercise more understanding or generosity in your next encounter.

While compassion helps us forge deeper connections, it's important to keep in mind that connection is a three-way street. We can't be disconnected from ourselves and still connect with others. We can't be a helper only to others, and we can't be only a helpee, benefiting from someone else's compassion. Healthy, strong relationships include extending compassion, receiving compassion, and practicing self-compassion.

Offering help is vital. We want strong relationships because they enrich our lives, create better work environments, and (from a selfish point of view) earn us social capital. Having impermeable boundaries is incompatible with having good working relations.

Receiving can often be a sticking point at work. Asking for help is smart. And there is strategy involved in knowing where to go for it, how to ask for it, and when to ask for it. Rejection is a key reason, particularly at work, that we don't reach out. We don't know what kind of support the other person wants, even if he is going through a crisis and we want to help. We don't know whether he wants to have a place where things seem normal and where he can have a break from the problem, and we don't want to overstep any boundaries. So we do nothing. We could, at the very least, tell the person that we realize he is going through a hard time, that we want to support him, and that we'll follow his lead on how best to do that.

In most cases, our work represents a symbiotic network—we aren't there alone, and we can't succeed alone. By necessity, organizations create roles to support efficiency—this is the definition of bureaucracy—but a humanized workplace acknowledges that people are more than their roles. We might rely on another person to complete tasks for us, and if we work in a big organization, we might not even know this person. Yet when we actively practice compassion, we can shift the narrow perspective that, say, views "Shauna in Contracts" as a person who didn't deliver the document we needed and instead see her as a person with a family, passions, stresses, and deadlines of her own. Simply moving from an instrumental perspective, where the other person is a means to an end, and seeing her in her fullness can make work relationships a lot happier and more productive.

Compassion is a worldview that sees the self and other in relationship, in connection. It is a reframing. Often when we are busy getting things done, it seems that the only thing that matters is the work and ourselves. Remembering that we are surrounded by real people is a reframing of our worldview from a negative, isolated default. And it makes us work better.

COMPASSION CREATES ACTION

Compassion does not negate our ability to remember that we have obligations to our customers, employees, and shareholders and that we need to do the best we can in our work. Repeat business relies on reputation and respect. And there are ways to be profitable without using practices that are harmful to others.

In 2012, Jeff Weiner, CEO of LinkedIn,[8] wrote a blog piece about compassion that went viral and put him on the map of the compassion discussion (which was rising to the height of its vogue at the time). In 2013, I attended a Wisdom 2.0 event where he spoke on the topic of compassion in the workplace. One of the most important points he made (in my opinion) was about the difference between compassion and empathy:

> *Through reading the book* The Art of Happiness—*the teachings of the Dalai Lama as told to author Howard Cutler—I learned the difference between compassion, defined as walking a mile in another person's shoes, and empathy, which is feeling what another person feels. Though [they are] oftentimes used synonymously in Western culture, the contrast between the two is an important one. As the Dalai Lama explains, if you are walking along a trail and come upon a person who is being crushed by a boulder, an empathetic reaction would result in you feeling the same sense of crushing suffocation and render you unable to help. The compassionate reaction would put you in the sufferer's shoes, thinking this person must be experiencing horrible pain so you're going to do everything in your power to remove the boulder and alleviate their suffering.*

In other words, compassion empowers us to act, to help, to solve problems rather than simply feel what another person is feeling. As it relates to work, this means being able to see things from someone else's perspective and be able to puzzle through other points of view we may not agree with.

The distinction Weiner makes between compassion and empathy is borne out by the most recent neuroscience coming out of the Max Planck Institute in Berlin. There, Tania Singer's work offers evidence that the "signature" in a person's brain (i.e., the pattern of neural activation, or brain activity, you can see in an fMRI) is different when a person is experiencing compassion versus empathy. The lead researcher in the study, Olga Klimecki, pointed to the importance of empathy in understanding others and their emotions but spoke of a downside to being empathic: if we feel the suffering of others too much, we experience emotional burnout. "Through compassion training," Klimecki says, "we can increase our resilience and approach stressful situations with more positive affect."

Singer and Klimecki also identified the tendency to be egocentric as innate in human beings, but found that there is a part of the brain, the right supramarginal gyrus, that recognizes a lack of empathy and autocorrects. This area of the brain helps us distinguish our own emotional state from that of other people and is responsible for empathy and compassion. When it doesn't function properly, or when we have to make particularly quick decisions, our capacity for empathy, the researchers found, is dramatically reduced. Given the quick decisions we need to make all the time at work, it is easy to see how this part of the brain doesn't autocorrect the way it should, limiting our ability to be compassionate.

Not long ago, I invited Scott Kriens, the billionaire former CEO of world-renowned tech company Juniper Networks, to speak to my class about how he had come to value compassion as a leadership skill. He explained that the idea of compassion first emerged for him after the loss of his father. The impact of that loss gave him an appreciation for other people's suffering. It also helped him see how suffering can challenge us to ask ourselves the "big" questions about authenticity and one's real purpose in their work.

When he finished talking about his experience, one of my students said, "Yeah, well it's easy for you to talk about the importance of compassion and honoring suffering when you were already a CEO, but do you honestly think you would have gotten where you got if this had been your motive along the way?"

At first, I was shocked at the question—for how blunt it was, the tone as much as the content. I worried that Scott would be offended. But rather than responding defensively, he considered the question and said that he didn't agree that compassion was a luxury for the already successful. He spoke about compassion and appreciation for the talents of team members as the key differentiator for successful teams and for successful leaders. He made the point that a company like Juniper Networks had brilliant talent, but so did a lot of other companies it was competing with. He said that the thing that would differentiate JN from other companies would be how well the teams worked together to solve problems. And this capacity was something that needed to be drawn out by a leadership that was respectful.

As we've seen, compassion isn't just about being "nice." In the workplace, it can take many forms, but at its heart is the notion that another person's perspective is, at minimum, valid—better yet, it is considered as equal to or primary to a self-centered analysis of a situation. Another person's growth, her feelings, her needs—all are in the mix as we interact with her or engage in behavior that directly or indirectly influences her. This is not always easy to put into practice, and is one of the reasons that compassion is tethered to wisdom. The traditional Buddhist articulation is a metaphor of the two wings of a bird. Both are needed, and are key parts of enlightened activity. It is hard for us to know what is best for another person, and there's nothing worse than justifying bad behavior as being in another person's interest.

Work is where we spend our time. If we let our values slide while we are there, we won't have them to return to at the end of the day when we get home. Our workplaces are part of our communities. We need to enact the kind of environment we want to live in while we're at work, one of not just tolerance and civility or putting up with one another but also respect and understanding. To do this, we need to find concrete, actionable ways to bridge differences with our colleagues. We can't get away with staying in the small circles of people with whom we are at ease. By definition, to get our work done, we need to stretch ourselves and deal with people who challenge and even offend us. We need to work with the people on our teams whom we are afraid of, or whom we are nervous about offending. And we need to do this not just to be good, compassionate people, but also because getting our work done requires it.

In addition to the practical benefits of compassion, I would argue that there remains a bigger argument for practicing compassion at work: because it is the right thing to do and because it matters to us as human beings if we don't do it. No matter the example we see in our national politics of incivility, we need to do better, to act as we would want our children to act. Values are irrelevant if they do not guide action. Ethics get strengthened when we practice them in the day-to-day. Only then will we be ready when and if a big moment comes. In the meantime, we can take pride in the notion that the small daily actions we take are moving the world in a better direction.

COMPASSION CAN BE TAUGHT

Some people worry that if, all of a sudden, they begin to focus their compassion on the needs of people on a global scale, they'll have to abnegate their responsibilities to the people they see every day. But compassion toward strangers does not dilute our love for our loved ones. After all, it's not a zero-sum game; nor is it a family-versus-others dichotomy. Just as a mother with more than one child is capable of loving all her children, so we can learn, through cultivation, to widen our circle of concern and extend compassion to an ever-expanding field. We don't have to view it as an all-or-nothing proposition—it's not that we are either Gandhi or the Dalai Lama or not on the map at all.

Research in neuroscience is increasingly suggesting that "use it or lose it" applies equally well to our neurons as to our muscles. The same is true of compassion. Qualities such as compassion are analogous to muscles, which, if trained, can be developed and strengthened.

So what are these skills exactly? Here's a brief overview of some of the skills I emphasize to my students when we study compassion.

- Developing awareness of our feelings and needs and the needs of others.

- Developing insight and understanding of how our mind works, why we feel what we feel, and how our patterns of thinking become stories about other people and the world.

- Developing motivation to be caring toward ourselves and others, and to reduce suffering.

- Developing an accepting/curious, noncondemning, and non-submissive orientation toward ourselves and others.

- Developing abilities to tolerate rather than avoid difficult feelings, memories, or situations.

- Not giving ourselves the benefit of the doubt when it comes to bias; not being too critical with ourselves.

- Developing mindful attention and using our attention to draw on helpful, compassionate images and/or a compassionate sense of self.

- Learning to plan and engage in compassionate behaviors that move us (and others) forward toward our (or their) life goals—to flourish.

- Having the courage/willingness to adopt a compassionate perspective even when it feels counterintuitive or we'd rather skip it.

Connecting across Differences

We see and interpret the same thing in different ways from our neighbor, and what we see and hear is significantly impacted by who we are and how we are influenced by our background and life experiences. Our differences inform how we perceive, interpret, speak, and listen. Life experiences, the cultures of the country we were raised in, our race, gender, and ethnicity—all these show up and influence our conversations. We also have habits of stereotyping other people, whether we want to or not, and these are also influenced by our culture and personal history. This use of categories to interpret the world, to stereotype other people, starts when we are toddlers and doesn't end automatically when we are grown-ups, even if we would like it to.

Yet we know that diverse workplaces perform better. According to a 2016 study conducted by global management consulting firm McKinsey and Company:

Companies that exhibit gender and ethnic diversity are, respectively, 15 percent and 35 percent more likely to outperform those that don't. And research indicates that organizations with more racial and gender diversity bring in more sales revenue, more customers, and higher profits.

Diversity also matters at the top: McKinsey found that companies in the top quartile of executive-board diversity had returns on equity that were 53 percent higher than those in the bottom quartile. Moreover, organizations with more female executives are more profitable, according to a 2016 analysis of more than 20,000 firms in 91 countries.[9]

Most of us want to relate to people who are different from us, but it is not always clear how, especially when stereotypes get in our way or we are afraid of being insulting or looking ignorant without meaning to.

We know that gender and race equality in the workplace is still slow in coming. The 2016 Women in the Workplace[10] survey found that, in the corporations surveyed, women made up only 19 percent of the highest-level executive officer positions (that is, CEO, CFO, and COO positions). When women try to negotiate for promotions or raises, they are 30 percent more likely to be seen as pushy or "aggressive." Not surprisingly, for every 100 women promoted to a management position, 130 men are promoted. Men of color are in a similar position, and fare worse than white women in some cases. Only 13 percent of senior management positions go to men of color, while white women hold a 27 percent share. When it comes to the C-suite, men of color and white women are closer, but men of color make up only 10 percent of positions, compared to 17 percent for white women. Women of color fare the worst, making up only 3 percent of C-suite positions and 8 percent of senior management positions. Considering the fact that women of color make up 38.2 percent of the female population, these statistics are abysmal.

There are obstacles to creating diversity in the first place, problems that start even before the biases in recruiting and hiring, and that can be traced back to when the career goals of children are formed. And even if an organization somehow manages to hire a diversity of team members, the next seriously nontrivial hurdle is to create enough psychological safety that people are comfortable speaking up and participating.

In terms of diversity, another important lesson in mindfulness/compassion/self-compassion is that different cultures "do" communication differently. In my work with students taking the Touchy-Feely course, I've found that they have a hard time not penalizing people from other cultures, even unconsciously. An exercise done in a T-group session (a small, intimate group of twelve students) about interpersonal influence invites each group member to rank the other members by having them line up in order of how much influence he or she perceives those people having on the rest of the group. Time and again, international students and women find themselves ranked at the bottom—and are understandably extremely upset as a result.

Yet when the micro-environment of the T-group is translated into the dominant real-world patterns of marginalizing women and non-whites, it is challenging for people to recognize that this is happening, let alone to correct the problem. The good news is that this outcome could be used as a vivid illustration of the kind of unconscious bias we all need to deal with in the world: We have to practice communication, continually, in community, and with honest and empathetic feedback. We cannot wall off our professional self from the reality of other people's real-life experiences and personal histories with suffering. When we are biased against other people, we are less able to respond to them.

What gets in the way of seeing people as deserving of compassion? In 1973, social psychologists John Darley and Daniel Batson[11] recruited sixty-seven students from the Princeton Theological Seminary to participate in the now-classic Good Samaritan Study, which looked at people's responsiveness to someone in an emergency situation. First, participants completed personality questionnaires on their religion. Then the researchers had some participants discuss potential jobs suitable for seminary graduates, while others discussed the parable of the Good Samaritan. Later, the participants began experimental procedures in one building and were then told to go to another building to continue. The researchers varied the level of urgency with which the groups were sent to the other building, and the task they would complete once they got there. Some participants were told they were late for the next task and needed to hurry; others were told that the assistant was ready for them now; and the rest, that they had a few minutes but they should head on over anyway. So participants were made to experience a high, medium, or low level of urgency.

On the way over to the next building, participants encountered a person doubled over in physical distress. Overall, 40 percent offered some help to that person. In low-urgency situations, 63 percent helped; in medium urgency, 45 percent; and in high-urgency situations, only 10 percent. Some even stepped over the man. In short, the degree to which they felt rushed impacted their decision to help. The nature of the task they were moving toward (even if the task was to give a sermon on the parable of the Good Samaritan) did not make a difference.

There was no correlation between "religious type" and helping behavior. The only variable that had some effect was "religion as a quest." Of the people who helped, those who saw religion as a quest were less likely to offer substantial help than those who scored low on this statement. Later analysis revealed that this might not have been caused by actual religious differences. The first requirement for compassion is to recognize suffering; it is possible that if people are rushing or distracted, they don't recognize suffering. The first step, therefore, is making the appraisal that someone needs and deserves compassion.

A decision made by Hancock Bank in New Orleans is an example of how sometimes compassion is understood as responsiveness. In 2005, after Hurricane Katrina, people had no way to get money from their accounts. The bank therefore started handing out paper IOUs to people in the community, to the tune of a couple of million dollars, so that they could meet their basic needs, such as food and water. This never would have been approved in a board room, but it was the responsive thing to do, but when we respond to need, we end up doing things we might not have planned. The vast majority of the money was repaid. Think of the spirit of civic engagement this brought to the bank and the community. The bank couldn't have set up a more effective public relations campaign.

Perspective taking is the key to (tactical and also ethical) problem solving, social skills, empathy, and overcoming conscious and unconscious bias against those who aren't in our group. Perspective taking is the ability to suspend one's perspective and (try to) see a situation from another person's point of view. It can mean being able to consider what that person is thinking and feeling and, on a subtler level, *why* he is thinking and feeling that way. We often do this automatically— when we consider the best way to give directions to someone from out of town (e.g., we give more specific and detailed directions than we would to a local). In other words, there isn't a sharp line between the cognitive skill of perspective taking and the holistic ability to think/feel/act with others in mind.

We develop the capacity for perspective taking typically around the age of two, when we figure out that our agenda (what we need and want) is not the only one that matters. Our mother's or sibling's agenda, for example—about the food we want to eat or the toys we want to play with—may differ from our own. This ability to understand others' perspectives as separate from our own happens to coincide with the time that we begin to develop a capacity for empathy and are able to relate to others' feelings and emotions in a meaningful way.

Like toddlers, sometimes we resist shifting our perspective to include other people's experiences. In the workplace, the drive to satisfy our own wants and needs may seem to outweigh those of others. But children who learn effective perspective taking have better social and problem-solving skills than those who don't. The same is true for grown-ups: with perspective taking, we can more effectively motivate others, successfully solve problems, collaborate, and offer effective feedback. We can create workplaces that have fewer pain points.[12]

5

Dealing with Ourselves

TOO MANY PEOPLE OVERVALUE WHAT THEY ARE NOT AND UNDERVALUE
WHAT THEY ARE.

—Malcolm S. Forbes

Several years ago, after completing four hundred days and one six-month program as part of traditional Tibetan teacher training, I went through a bit of a disaster phase. I was ABD ("all but dissertation"), a stage where many better doctoral candidates than I stall out for good. In addition to trying to finish my dissertation, I had a one-year-old, I was grieving the death of my father, and I was working full time at the Stanford Compassion Center as the inaugural director of education. I was so harried in this two-year period that I wasn't taking care of myself in the most basic ways. (I gained fifty pounds and rarely slept more than five hours a night.) One day, I was checking my e-mail on my phone as I made my way to a budget meeting when I saw a message in my in-box that made me stop in my tracks. It was from a colleague writing to say that he'd missed me in class the day before and hoped that everything was okay.

My heart raced. I opened my calendar and, sure enough, I had been scheduled as a guest lecturer that night. I had completely forgotten to show up, or even cancel. My face flushed, and fears of my fundamental incompetence flooded my mind. I had to bike to my meeting across campus, and those feelings chased me the whole ride. How could I have done something like this? How could this have happened? How could I be so careless?

By the time I left the meeting an hour later and headed to nurse my daughter during my lunch hour, the initial shock had worn off, but I was still feeling unsettled. It wasn't until my sister called me, on her lunch break at the hospital where she works, that the irony, and humor, of the situation became obvious. I told her what had happened: that I had forgotten to show up to offer a lecture on self-compassion for a course taught by the world-renowned forgiveness expert Fred Luskin, and I'd been beating myself up all morning.

We laughed until we were in hysterics. After I hung up the phone, I felt some measure of relief, and had the composure to e-mail Fred and apologize. (For the record, Fred wrote back and said that he understood.)

We all have stories like this, of intense mortification, the kind where you want the earth (somewhere in the lower mantle if not the inner core) to magically open up so you can jump in and hide, possibly forever. I realized from this experience that applying self-compassion in professional contexts is a double black diamond maneuver, and that if I weren't able to master the skill, I would spend the rest of my life (both professional and personal) in abject misery.

The next time I lectured on self-compassion, I took this experience with me and shared it with the class—because it's one thing to talk about self-compassion in theory, but quite another to practice it when the shit truly hits the fan.

What Is Self-Compassion?

When I talk to people about self-compassion, their first reaction is often one of concern or disbelief. They think that being kind to themselves will make them weak or complacent; they believe that self-criticism keeps them accountable or improves their performance; and they worry that letting go of the habit of self-criticism will somehow render them less capable. What they don't know is that the opposite is true: beating themselves up and holding themselves accountable to unattainable standards are actually very likely to undermine their performance.

Recent research[1] indicates that self-criticism predicts depression, avoidance behaviors (such as trying to avoid failure), loss of self-esteem, negative perfectionism (maladaptive perfectionism, the unhelpful perfectionism that doesn't drive us toward better performance but, rather, toward shame and anxiety), procrastination, and rumination. Ultimately, self-criticism compromises your goals and undermines your pursuits, whether they are academic, health related, personal, or professional.

Research on self-compassion, however, shows that it is unequivocally correlated with mental well-being, including less stress, anxiety, depression, or perfectionism. Positive qualities such as happiness, greater motivation, greater self-responsibility, healthier lifestyle choices, and better interpersonal relationships are all boosted by self-compassion. In the context of health care, where there are extremely high rates of stress and burnout, research points to self-compassion as a capacity that lessens the level of stress people experience (perceived stress) and, as a result, improves the quality of care they are able to offer. The inevitable negative experiences and emotions of life don't go away when someone is self-compassionate, but the response to those emotions and experiences changes. By relating to rather than avoiding these negative or uncomfortable feelings, greater well-being is able to emerge.

Self-compassion engenders resilience; it empowers you to be nimble and flexible, and gives you the ability to identify problems, accept negative feedback from others, and change habits that no longer serve you. (In Silicon Valley parlance, it enables you to "pivot.") This type of openness to change and resilience to setbacks helps you grow, learn, form good habits, and, ultimately, be more successful.

To many, the idea that self-compassion can make us more competitive in the workplace is counterintuitive to say the least. So many of us have internalized the idea that excellence is a result of not just discipline but self-flagellation, that the idea of being "easy" on ourselves is a scary one. But studies show that self-compassion meditation actually enhances willpower and our ability to stick with behavioral change goals. This is a point I've picked up on from my friend and colleague from CCARE, Kelly McGonigal, who introduced me to Claire Adams's (Louisiana State University) and Mark Leary's (Duke University) tantalizing Donut Study.[2]

In the study, college-age women were first given a glass of water, then a "forbidden food" of one of two varieties of donuts. Everyone watched a video about rain forests while drinking the water and eating the donut. One group of women heard the following script from a researcher: "You might wonder why we picked donuts to use in the study. It's because people sometimes eat unhealthy, sweet foods while they watch TV. We thought it would be more like the 'real world' to have people eat a dessert or junk food. But several people have told me that they feel bad about eating donuts in this study, so I hope you won't be hard on yourself. Everyone eats unhealthily sometimes, and everyone in this study eats this stuff, so I don't think there's any reason to feel really bad about it. This little amount of food doesn't really matter anyway. Just wait a second and I'll bring you the questionnaire." The other group of women received no such guidance.

Both groups of women were then told to try at least one of each of three bowls of candy (Reese's Peanut Butter Cups, Skittles, and York Peppermint Patties) and to complete a questionnaire about their favorites. They were welcome to eat as much candy as they wanted while they filled out their forms, and there was plenty available in the lab. Who do you think ate more candy, the women who had been told they shouldn't feel bad about eating junk food or those that didn't get this message?

You've probably guessed it: the women who were compassionate with themselves about their indulgence indulged less. Those who received the message from the researcher ate 28 grams of candy, compared to 70 grams for the women who received no such message. The women who were not practicing self-compassion ate more than twice as much as their peers.

Not only does this study clearly illustrate the link between will-power and self-compassion, but it also provokes some interesting questions about the role of self-criticism and self-compassion from a management perspective. What kinds of feedback yield the best results for employees, and how can managers best respond to setbacks and failures? Does normalizing a setback for a teammate or a direct report encourage future screwups or provide a springboard for talking about what went wrong and how to prevent it from happening again? The research suggests we'll do better with the second approach.

Ultimately, self-compassion is best understood as a subtype of compassion. The healthiest attitude is one in which we don't exclude ourselves from our concern, or judge ourselves ever more harshly than we would our worst enemy. But self-compassion should not be confused with selfishness. Obsessing about our own pain to the exclusion of caring about others is not the point. As with all important things in life, there needs to be a balance. Self-compassion means applying the same compassion to self and others, including ourselves in the equation, but not valuing ourselves more than anyone else. Remember, compassion connects us to our common humanity. At the end of the day, we are one person on a planet of billions. Denying that we matter is ultimately another form of self-preoccupation.

In the traditional curriculum for compassion training, self-compassion wasn't recognized as its own discipline. Dr. Kristin Neff at the University of Texas, Austin, is the wonder woman who first conducted empirical research on self-compassion and developed the instrument that is used around the world to measure it.[3] Neff says that self-compassion is a challenge for most people, just as it was a challenge for her. The idea that you're "allowed to be nice to yourself," as she put it, was a revelation for her. Out of this insight, she developed a training program and an eight-week course that has been of tremendous benefit to thousands of people.

Her self-compassion measurement scale is comprised of three elements. First, self-compassion is predicated on mindfulness of your own suffering. This includes recognizing your physical pain, illness, stress, difficult emotions, difficult situations, negative thoughts, disappointments, as well as the underlying need or desire to be healthy, to be happy, to connect with others, and to do well or do good. The second is common humanity, or an understanding that your suffering does not mean there is something uniquely wrong with you and your life, that it is, rather, part of the human condition. We all have pain, we all blow it from time to time, we are all works in progress. Finally, treating yourself with self-kindness eliminates the impulse to beat yourself up all the time.

When I teach this material in workplace settings or to veterans with PTSD, I highlight self-coaching over self-kindness. Self-coaching has a stronger feel to it than self-kindness—the term "coaching" seems to leave more room for error when compared to self-kindness. This isn't to diminish the importance of self-kindness, but the idea of self-kindness can be off-putting for many of us, and sometimes we need to be a strong advocate for accountability with ourselves. One of the exercises my students find powerful is to take a situation they feel caught in and to visualize that a friend in this exact situation has come to them seeking advice. In the visualization, they walk through exactly how they would support this friend, both what they would say and the attitude they would take toward her. Then I instruct them to repeat the process, but directing it toward themselves. Yes, it is artificial and awkward—and it works like a charm. Learning to coach ourselves through suffering requires sticking with ourselves in it. It also requires some tough love. Tough love is an important skill to cultivate, but it is still love—and it is different from self-deprecation.

The Two Arrows

One of the traditional wisdom stories from Buddhism is called "The Arrow." The story starts with the Buddha asking monastics what the difference is between a practitioner of mindfulness and a nonpractitioner. The monastics don't answer but, instead, challenge the Buddha to answer his own question. The Buddha suggests that when nonpractitioners experience pain, they will "grieve, lament, beat their breast, become distraught. So they feel two pains, physical and mental."

The metaphor the Buddha uses is being shot by not one but two arrows. The first arrow is the pain itself. That's part of life, unavoidable. The second arrow is the "resistance-obsession" we pile onto that pain. We obsess over it, or we hide from it, distracting ourselves, avoiding it at all costs. There is no escape from the first arrow; the second arrow is avoidable. The practitioner of mindfulness feels the first arrow but not the second.

Choosing not to resist, not to avoid the pain but, rather, to face it head-on, is the way around that arrow. As one student put it, "I work myself into a frenzy—when I have one negative thought, I think about another thing that is going wrong or might go wrong. It's like a waterfall of negative emotions." So many of us suffer, truly suffer, from this type of narrow attention on the negative. Throughout our day, we are shot repeatedly by our aches, pains, regrets, disappointments, insecurities, and failures, throwing at ourselves not just one arrow or two, but dozens, hundreds, thousands. Self-compassion is the anti-dote to this unnecessary suffering. We feel stressed, and we want to avoid the stress, so we get involved with an off-topic or less important activity. Or we "cyberloaf"—yes, cyberloafing is a researched thing[*]— and cost employers billions of dollars in lost productivity.[4]

Self-compassion requires that we be vulnerable, which is uncom-fortable for a lot of us, especially in a workplace setting. But being uncomfortable is a necessary part of both personal and professional growth. We can't fire the parts of ourselves we aren't happy with. It's important that we engage with the discomfort of looking at our mis-takes and what led to them. To do a real recon on ourselves requires courage, accountability, and vulnerability.

Many of us tend to intellectualize tough experiences or deflect awk-ward moments with humor or cynicism. But joking and deflecting don't allow us to be open to the new experiences and thought processes that will allow us to grow. As one of my teachers told me when I was on a retreat as a nineteen-year-old, "If you can't be cheesy, you can't be free." And he was right—if we spend our time avoiding looking bad or soft, we can't express a range of emotions. We can't be authentic.

For a lot of us, allowing ourselves to experience the full range of emotions at work is a stretch. And stretching mentally, just like stretch-ing our bodies, requires moving past our comfort zone and into un-known, riskier territory. It takes guts to realize that our old ways aren't serving us. But beating up on ourselves, avoiding situations where we might look bad, or compartmentalizing negative emotions limits

---

[*] http://esource.dbs.ie/bitstream/handle/10788/2074/hdip_woods_f_2014.pdf?se.

our ability for self-awareness and personal growth. Being vulnerable doesn't mean that you have to check your caution or humor at the door; it just means that you allow yourself to feel things, sometimes unpleasant or uncomfortable things. Anyone on a path that involves truth and self-knowledge and growth has been challenged, has felt that he can't see the end and can't go back to the beginning again. It's like once you've seen something, you can't unsee it. When you start to go down this path, it is difficult to turn back.

There is a story that has been repeated for about thirty years among Tibetan Buddhist practitioners of Chögyam Trungpa, the controversial figure who pioneered adapting Tibetan Buddhism in America in the 1960s. As legend has it (and as corroborated by Judith Simmer-Brown, distinguished professor of contemplative and religious studies at Naropa University and a lead teacher in the community Trungpa started), Trungpa would begin his teachings on more than one occasion by saying to the crowd of patchouli-wearing hippies gathered around him, "If you are new here, go home! Because once you start down this path, there is only one way out. And that is to walk it to its completion."

His point was that the practices he was teaching really do change the way we see the world. And then we are called by this perspective shift to some kind of action. We won't be able to start and then unstart. Once we develop the capacity for mindfulness, we can't unsee our patterns. The only way to deal with them, then, is to rework them—and doing that is not for the faint of heart.

THE FIRST ARROW: ENCOUNTERING SHAME

The workplace is a perfect storm of shame. Sometimes it happens because we messed up (as in objectively made a mistake or dropped the ball). Maybe I forgot that I was supposed to plan an event or create and send out the agenda for a meeting. Maybe I forgot to order an

ingredient for the kitchen or supplies for the classroom, and everyone is showing up in five minutes and there's no stuff. Maybe I forgot
to show up for a guest lecture on self-compassion. There are multiple
permutations of mortification.

Jeanne Tsai,[5] a psychology professor at Stanford and director of the
Culture and Emotion Lab, researches shame as an emotion pertinent
to our identities and mental health. In her work, she has been particularly interested in how cultural influences make us feel ashamed. In
her comparative research between Western and East Asian contexts,
she has come to see that there are different versions of shame, specifically individual and collective. Shame is a problem in the West as
well as the East, but predominantly for different reasons, which she
attributes to differing cultural values. In the West, Tsai finds that we
experience the greatest shame when we fall short as individuals. In
East Asian contexts, shame is more readily evoked when one's family
or organization is let down.

While Tsai's work offers fascinating insight into the different types
of shame people experience within various cultural contexts, the
most profound insight I take away from it is that there are multiple
types of shame, and these different types of shame are evoked from
different circumstances and different facets of ourselves. We feel deeply
distraught when we let ourselves or others down. At the same time,
living up to all the demands and expectations placed on us is an impossibility.

At work in particular, opportunities for both types of shame
abound. After all, even in the most competitive, highly individualistic
work environments, we can't be 100 percent focused only on our own
success. If we are getting paid for our work, by definition someone else
must need it, must value it, and therefore their opinion of our work and
of us matters. Work is fundamentally an exchange, and this makes it
a social, interactive endeavor that includes the needs of ourselves and
others. We have the reality of shared bottom lines, objective deliver-

ables. We want to do well ourselves, so that we have opportunities to grow, to take on responsibility, and to earn more money, and we are ashamed when we fall short of these goals (or if others progress faster than we do).

If we work in an environment that is centered around individual rewards, such as bonuses and promotions, we'll be incentivized to feel ashamed when we mess up as individuals. If we work in an environment that emphasizes collective success and incentivizes that the team rise or fall together, our attention will be directed to mistakes that impact the group's success. In this environment, when we let the group down, we feel ashamed.

When we are feeling inadequate in any situation, we tend to compare ourselves to others. This is a common response but not a helpful one, and serves only to further shame us. One of my students described his instinct to compare himself to others with an inner dialogue that goes something like this: "Everyone else is so smart and accomplished and really knows what they're doing. There's no way I'll ever be as successful as so-and-so, no matter how hard I try. I'm an imposter."

While many of us believe our self-criticism drives our success, this type of self-criticism is counterproductive. We equate self-compassion with sugarcoating the problem rather than dealing with it. We see it as letting ourselves off the hook. After all, isn't feeling ashamed an important motivator for not making the same mistake twice? Isn't that all-consuming bad feeling we get when we've messed up in effect a visceral reminder of what matters, something that serves an important function, demanding our attention when we've lost track of our purpose? Isn't the gnawing guilt that creeps in when we do less than our best a kind of important feedback? A built-in compass to help keep us on track?

Workplaces don't exist for our personal growth and self-reflection. When we're at work, our actions impact other people, our choices matter. (They matter outside work, too, but that's not the topic we're discussing here.) An "I'm learning from it and growing as a person or really getting insight into my wounded inner child" approach to an important task won't cut it. We need to deliver the deliverables. We are accountable to our coworkers and clients, to our mission, and we have to produce work that is up to shared standards. So isn't it appropriate to feel bad when we blow it?

There is a clear and helpful distinction between guilt and shame. Guilt, while unpleasant, can help us pay attention to a transgression or broken commitment and can ideally precipitate fixing these ruptures. Shame, on the other hand, is an emotional response to the way we feel about ourselves. It is not productive. It keeps us tied up in our own negative experience about what we've done and gets in the way of our ability to respond, learn, and repair. The distinction between the two is subtle but important, but with intention and awareness we can pinpoint when we've tipped over from productive self-reflection and into the extra layer of self-preoccupation.

The upside of guilt (what I prefer to call remorse) comes into play when it functions as a moral compass. Remorse is productive when it serves as a signpost that something is off. It prevents us from losing track of our commitments and values, our intention and purpose. It exposes those moments when our integrity has been broken, allowing us to restore it with ourselves and others. Remorse flags for us that there's a problem.

Remorse is also the coaching we can offer ourselves when we're holding back our best effort. It brings out what my teacher Lama Willa calls our "no-nonsense self," the part of us that cuts through our excuses and gets shit done. Like an athletic coach giving a pep talk before a big game, this can be an intense push, but it is supportive and, ultimately, motivational. The coach in this analogy stands for us doing what has to be done as an expression of our higher purpose. It is embodied in many wisdom traditions as a spiritual warrior, the archetype who steps up and gets even the most challenging things done to make the world a better place.

When we are mindful, we can remind ourselves that we have the ability to feel or think something without identifying with it. We might feel we've done something badly, for example, but that does not mean *we* are bad. We can also remind ourselves that a willingness to feel the sting of feedback or constructive criticism is part of the process of growing, of embodying a growth mind-set. Compassion reminds us that these are feelings that people everywhere go through when they get difficult feedback, and that like them, we are up to the task of sticking with it, getting through it. And as we get better at practicing these skills and grow wiser and more capable, we will be better able to do this—not to mention better able to support people around us in doing the same. With the willingness to feel discomfort, we can accept that things aren't perfect but can be improved. All this starts with an honest assessment of what's not working. And this is precisely what self-compassion as a mind-set, as a practice, can be so effective at addressing.

THE SECOND ARROW: NEGATIVE SCRIPTS

My business is going to fail. I am a total sham.

So many people have tried to do the same thing I'm trying to do and failed. Why would I succeed?

I'm not smart enough to do this!

How could I have been so stupid?

How did you feel reading the comments above? Did any of them resonate with you? If so, then you are already familiar with the sting of the second arrow. Sentiments like these often enter our minds when we're feeling inadequate or nervous. When they become repetitive thought loops, when we get caught in their circular illogic, psychologists call them "scripts." From an early age, we internalize these scripts from influential people in our families (parents, siblings) and communities (teachers, friends). Then we go through life repeating them to ourselves without stopping to think about where they originated. Most of the time, we don't even realize we're doing it.

In some ways, this impulse to turn inward when things go wrong is useful—it focuses our attention on what went wrong. The problem is that negative scripts don't help us view ourselves or the problem from a perspective that will lead to solutions or improvement. A bad situation won't get any better if we call ourselves names. Beating up on ourselves is different from constructively coaching ourselves to understand what went wrong so we can solve it (or mitigate its aftershocks) and then avoid making a similar mistake in the future.

The good news is that when we realize we're replaying a script, we have the option to rewrite it. This takes time, patience, and practice—it doesn't happen at the flip of a switch. Still, it is well worth the effort because the alternative is to continue playing these negative, destructive scripts over and over as the bad soundtrack to our lives.

Accomplish This: Accelerator Moment

Rewriting the Script

Many of us don't realize that we have repetitive loops playing in our heads. These scripts have been a part of us for so long that we may have gotten used to them and stopped noticing them. The next time you are confronted with something stressful, take a moment to notice where your mind goes. Notice the thoughts and beliefs that arise and continue to play over and over. Isolate this loop, come up with another story you'll tell yourself when you encounter a similar challenge—flip the script!—and practice bringing this new story to mind when you feel frustrated, embarrassed, or challenged by a situation.

When the negative script starts its loop, it's tough to think clearly. Instead of coaching ourselves through the moment, we sometimes look to a trusted friend, sibling, coworker, life coach, therapist, spouse, or parent to prop us up. This is a natural instinct and, in part, a logical desire to connect and get support from those close to us. The problem is that these other people aren't always available when we need them, and if we go to them too often, we become a drag on them. Or, as is the case sometimes, they offer us the wrong kind of support, and we become even more frustrated, with them and ourselves as a result. The reality is that even if we have a great support network that offers wise counsel, at the end of the day we're still the ones who need to act on the advice. And the more we rely on other people to guide us or prop us up, the less able we are to cultivate resilience and acquire new skills.

Sometimes, the negative voice in our head is so loud we just want to hide. Confiding in anyone feels risky and intensifies our shame, so we go into isolation, afraid we've just proven to ourselves, and the world, that our worst fears about ourselves are actually true. We might take a sick day, avoid the people impacted by our problem, or even switch jobs to outrun the shame. It is such a big problem that the Centers for Disease Control and Prevention deems it a health risk. In fact, in 2015, the CDC reported that "productivity losses linked to absenteeism cost employers $225.8 billion annually in the United States, or $1,685 per employee."[6]

Embedded in the desire to hide out is an adaptive, logical response:

the impulse to find space to self-soothe and regroup. This is different from hiding out to avoid the difficult feelings and potential fallout from the mistake, or trying to cover the problem up rather than address it. Paradoxically, though, when we avoid the situation to make it go away, we actually increase the perceived severity of the problem. We have to go back to work eventually, and if the problem is in an unpleasant interpersonal dynamic we are contributing to, it will show up at our next job as well.

Even if we don't physically hide out, we can check out mentally. We are at work but don't really care; we aren't invested in the outcome. We're going through the motions; or we're living our life in the future, waiting for our next vacation to come, ignoring the day-to-day and the people around us. It can be tempting to numb ourselves to the people and events around us, telling ourselves that we don't care. But this not only stunts our performance but also diminishes our experience of our own lives. We zone out at work, but then we can't stop zoning out when we get home—the ambivalence follows us.

THE FIRST ARROW: FEELING OVERWHELMED

Overwhelm is a painful and ubiquitous workplace problem, and it often goes hand in hand with shame. The causes for overwhelm are many—we might feel this way when we didn't finish what we were supposed to do and are now going to get found out. Or we did the task but we did a crappy job. Or we might feel overwhelmed in anticipation of a time crunch coming down the pike. Or by life impinging on work—we've got a deadline, and our parent or spouse is sick. Or the combination of life and work and all the million things that need to get done in both domains and the fact that there are just not enough hours in the day to tend to both.

While we may not be able to change the number of demands on our time, we can change how we respond to this feeling of overwhelm.

And that response can determine how much additional pain we experience and how badly we are debilitated by it.

THE SECOND ARROW: PILING IT ON

Many of us struggle to get around to doing the things that are the most important to us. We can't face the sum total of the demands on us and become paralyzed, or we focus on the ones that are least important. We write an e-mail when we should be writing a report. We complain instead of just doing our work. There are many ways we make it worse for ourselves with counterproductive behavior.

For example, you are a few days away from a big deadline that can't be pushed back. You aren't ready; you're not even halfway there. Now what? When we are overwhelmed by how much we have to do, it can be tempting to multitask. Yet, as it's impossible to actually do more than one thing at a time well, we end up switching among tasks and being incredibly unproductive. The costs of task switching are enormous: our productivity becomes minuscule. We're trying to do everything and doing it all half-assed.

We also self-sabotage by complaining, going on and on about how busy we are. Or someone asks us to have coffee or take a walk, and we launch into a rant about the enormity of our to-do list. This usually just makes us feel worse and more stressed out. The other person doesn't love it, either. The fact is that complaining about our situation to others or ourselves basically takes over whatever bandwidth we might have been able to turn toward getting stuff done. Obsessing about the problem makes us not only neurotic but self-absorbed, which feels terrible and is off-putting to others. It can work us up into a frenzy, an anxious, neurotic mess. Sometimes we can end up rehashing our issues until we get stalled out in depression

When we feel overwhelmed we often start vividly imagining worst-case scenarios. The technical term for this is *catastrophizing*, and it's a great word to keep in mind. It goes a step beyond worrying. As the cliché goes, we turn to praying for what we don't want to happen. When we feel that time is scarce, we logically try to cut corners, dropping basic self-care to create time. We tend to sleep less when we are overwhelmed. Many of us go to the gym less, eat crappier food. We don't spend the minute it takes to put our lunch in a bowl, eating it out of the takeout carton to "save time."

Or we do things to self-soothe that sound good in the moment but don't actually make us feel better. This is where the long tradition of the after-work drink comes from. We choose something that we believe will be soothing but that actually makes our situation worse in the long run.

What Does Work: Practicing Self-Compassion

We are all searching for ways to make our lives work, even if we go about our days very differently and are filling different roles. Everyone we are working with wants to provide for themselves and their family, feel valued, feel that their work matters. They want to avoid getting sick, and they don't want their loved ones to get sick. In short, as human beings, we have a shared quandary.

Identifying our shared quandary is the opposite of isolation, self-absorption, self-flagellation, and dysfunctional reliance on other people. It is the recognition that underneath all the differences among people, there are also important similarities. Choosing to draw on this shared quandary mind-set keeps us from feeling isolated or uniquely flawed. Instead of seeing our mistakes as evidence that the negative scripts are true, we can see them as what makes us human. We can face our mistakes with the recognition that, yes, we made these mistakes, but so has everyone else. We can accept accountability. We can acknowledge. We can problem-solve. We can apologize. But we don't need to hide out, because we know that other people can relate. They've also forgotten an appointment, been excluded, lost a client—you name it; they've experienced it. Welcome to the club.

One way to practice self-compassion is to find physical self-soothing techniques that work for you. When you are ashamed or overwhelmed, you can anchor yourself in your body in a way that not only comforts your mind, but helps down-regulate your physical response to stress. Becoming present in our bodies, therefore, is the antidote to spinning out.

There are many ways to do this, but one strategy Kristin Neff recommends is putting a hand on your heart while you recite a phrase of self-compassion. These phrases are the opposite of the negative scripts that typically take over our brains in moments of stress; they acknowledge our suffering without blame or recrimination. Experiment with self-compassion phrases such as:

This is a moment of suffering.
Suffering is part of life.
May I be kind to myself.
May I give myself the compassion I need.

If you aren't prepared to fully "go there," with a hand on your heart, find another prompt that works for you. Whatever method you choose, be a friend to yourself. Literally, *be there* for yourself, the way you would for a friend. Sometimes people find that picturing themselves as a child can naturally bring up more self-kindness than thinking of themselves today, in their adult incarnation.

Experiment with your own language and your own process. Crack the code by finding something physical that is nurturing to you. It might mean getting in a great workout at lunchtime, taking a quick walk, keeping a cozy sweater at your desk to wrap yourself in, or treating yourself to a soothing cup of tea. It could be as simple as putting in your earbuds and listening to your favorite playlist on Spotify—anything that feels comforting and nourishing to you.

Accomplish This: Self-Compassion

Practicing self-compassion is as important as practicing compassion with others. When cultivating self-compassion feels challenging, try the following approaches:

1. **Use lunch as an act of self-care.** When you eat, take a moment to notice this nourishment you're giving yourself. You have the power to choose to eat something that makes you feel good. Bonus: research shows that when you make a healthy food choice, noticing the positive feelings this gives you serves to reinforce the behavior, making you more likely to make healthy choices at the next meal.

2. **Remember that we all feel like frauds.** When you find yourself in self-deprecation mode, calling yourself names, telling yourself that you can't do something well enough, and generally being a bully to yourself, remember that most people suffer from "imposter syndrome"—the feeling that we are just pretending, that we don't really belong, that we will be found out, that our true inadequacy will become obvious to the people around us. The fact is that everyone you work with, no matter how self-assured they seem, experiences self-doubt. This is the human condition. And these are just thoughts, so you don't have to believe them.

3. **Be a friend to yourself.** As corny as that may sound, it's a trick my business school students have found incredibly useful. When you notice you're being hard on yourself over a problem, imagine a dear friend coming to you with the same problem. How

would you respond? How would you offer support? What would you say? How would you regard your friend? Now try giving these responses to yourself.

4. **Ask for help.** Many of us are caught up in the idea that we need to "be a professional," which we equate as being stoic, handling things on our own. In this mind-set, we don't think to ask for kindness or validation. In fact, we would likely refuse to accept it. Over time, though, this "I've got this" attitude begins to wear thin, and we realize we can't do our jobs alone. Experiment with giving someone else the chance to support you. If this is a completely foreign idea to you, then I suggest you do it even more. People *like* to help! Think of how you feel when you get to help others. Helping people makes us feel good about ourselves and connected to others. So, instead of defaulting to "No, thanks" or "It's okay, I'm fine" when someone offers you something, try saying yes. It took until I had my third child to be willing to allow a friend to put together a meal delivery list, because I was unwilling to ask for help. It was a breakthrough experience for me, and when I went back to work, I found that I was better able to ask for help when I felt overwhelmed by things, such as constructing the lab notebooks for my class. In that case, an administrative assistant happily stepped in and enjoyed the process whereas I was terrified of printing out stickers and figuring out how to attach them, not to mention the time it would take that I didn't have.

Self-Compassion and Self-Esteem

I first met Kristin Neff when I was invited to give a talk with her and CCARE's Kelly McGonigal for the Palo Alto Mothers Symposium. Neff began her path in research by focusing on self-esteem as a young doctoral student at UC Berkeley and found that, despite its popularity, self-esteem wasn't living up to its name. Over the years, psychologists—starting with Stanford's Albert Bandura in his research in the 1960s—developed something called observational learning, or social learning theory. Experiments were conducted in which children modeled another's behavior and then evaluated themselves based on how they compared. In short, self-esteem was considered a summary judgment of how valuable a person was. More specifically, that value was relational: I feel good if I am better than you. For decades, self-esteem was viewed as a key marker of well-being in children and a central goal in education and parenting strategies. But Neff's 2003 research revealed that self-esteem was not the silver bullet many believed it to be—and in fact, this central tenet of our educational systems may do more harm than good.

Fast-forward to what is now understood to be a narcissism epidemic among the generations who were served the most concentrated indoctrinations of self-esteem. From the 1980s to 2009, narcissism rates among college-age students doubled to 30 percent.[7] Narcissism is a disorder of self-preoccupation, seeing the world from a self-referential vantage point, one that doesn't include others. Narcissistic students focus not on learning but on how they are perceived, on feeling good about themselves only when they compare more favorably than others. They are stuck in a state of competition and view themselves from the outside. Eventually, when they rise to be surrounded by people who are at their level (in school, at work), they have no idea how to exist. Their whole sense of self is built on being the best, but they're not the best anymore (if they ever were). That makes it tough for them to connect with others and collaborate.

The self-esteem-based identity that believes "I'm able to be happy only if I'm uniquely good and actually better than others" follows us from childhood to college and eventually to work and into our adult relationships. We find ourselves in the untenable position of being threatened by our friends, team members, and colleagues. Success is framed as a zero-sum game. We don't want to bring on the most talented people; they might show us up. We'd be more likely to stab them in the back than side with them. This perspective is not conducive to strong social networks and collaborative success, the cornerstone of innovation. Nor is it beneficial to psychological health: according to current psychology, social comparison is basically one of the quickest routes to misery. If we view someone as more successful than we are, smarter, richer, or "better" in any way, it is going to make us feel "less than," unhappy. When we compare ourselves against others, we can't win. When we come out ahead in our own minds, we act like jerks and become isolated. When we come out behind, we feel terrible and are cut off as well.

The inevitability of "topping out" is a well-known problem at Stanford. The students here got in only because they were the best where they came from. But here they are surrounded by other people who were also the best. They can't *all* be the best anymore, yet they have no idea how to deal with life or themselves other than by being the best. So they are miserable, but pressured to pretend that all is well. This is often described as "duck syndrome": gliding along with seaming ease on the surface while paddling furiously to stay afloat. And part of what fuels their paddling is the shame and self-criticism under the surface.[*]

When we covered self-esteem and self-compassion in my course, one of my students wrote about his experiences in a reflection paper:

> *In my experience in the workplace people have generally empha-sized self-esteem over self-compassion. I think that this is a result of a number of factors. First, the workplace tends to be a com-petitive environment. There are a finite number of promotions*

---

[*] Further details on the difference between narcissism and self-esteem: www.leah weissphd.com/narcissim-vs-self-esteem.

that can be made, or a finite bonus pool that can be disbursed. Thus, managers and employees are inclined to use individualistic frameworks that help differentiate them from their peers.

Secondly, it empirically seems like people with high self-esteem are more likely to be leaders. Colleagues sense that an individual thinks highly of him- or herself and become interested in earning that person's validation. On the other hand, people who practice self-compassion are less visible in the workplace. The fact that these people are less visible makes it more difficult for managers and other colleagues to quickly find this "leadership" attribute.

While this student observes that self-esteem seems to be more valued in the workplace, practicing self-compassion does not in fact make workers invisible. It doesn't blind us to our shortcomings or make us dismissive of the areas we most need to develop. In fact, as research has demonstrated time and again, self-compassion does not lead to a life of complacency. But it does make us less self-centered and better able to cooperate with, learn from, and lead others.

6

The Wisdom of Emotions

BETWEEN STIMULUS AND RESPONSE THERE IS A SPACE. IN THAT SPACE IS
OUR POWER TO CHOOSE OUR RESPONSE. IN OUR RESPONSE LIES OUR
GROWTH AND OUR FREEDOM.

Viktor E. Frankl, *Man's Search for Meaning*[1]

A student of mine whom I'll call John told me the following story after class one day, when we were discussing losing our temper at work. He said that his biggest work meltdown of all time happened a few years ago, when he was on the phone with his business partner, whom he'd left in charge of operations for a few days while he was on vacation. When his partner called to relate a major problem that had occurred, John admitted, "I immediately attributed the issue to his carelessness and laziness. I got angrier than I've ever been and said some very hurtful things to him, and that was essentially the end of our business relationship."

In fact, John had been feeling uneasy about the direction of the company for a while and had had serious concerns about his business partner's declining work ethic. Yet, instead of dealing with those emotions as they occured, he had suppressed them, letting them burst forth only when a difficult situation occurred. As he said in class, he realized, looking back, that this was something he always did with uncomfortable emotions. He would either suppress them or distract himself from them. He told me, "I think the tuning that led to this explosion ties back to my tendency to suppress my emotions in life, but especially at work. Looking back on the experience, [I see that] if I had allowed myself to fully experience my fear and anger when the feelings first arrived and been curious and inquiring into the root of these feelings, I would have been able to address the underlying problem with my partner much sooner."

As it turns out, John's business partner had been battling depression, but instead of being compassionate toward him and mindful of his own feelings, John had let the situation degrade into something beyond repair and that served no one. He felt that if he had possessed better emotion-regulation skills, he would at least have been able to salvage the relationship and get his partner the emotional support he needed at the time.

John isn't the only person who has ever "snapped" at work. I have a friend who, after months of dealing with an abusive boss, finally stormed out of a meeting in front of her entire team when he yelled at her one time too many. Then there's the infamous JetBlue flight attendant who, after a particularly bad day, cursed at passengers, opened the emergency exit door while the plane was still on the tarmac, and slid out.[2] There's the baseball player who punches a wall in the locker room after a bad game and as a result loses use of his pitching arm. For every work situation, there is an example of someone losing his cool.

There are too many pain points at work to name them all. Anger, jealousy, scarcity, worry, dread, distraction or lack of focus, boredom, stress, paranoia, anxiety, feeling overwhelmed—the list goes on and on. Typically, "snapping" at work involves some form of emotional outburst—yelling, crying, slamming doors, storming off—though, in extreme cases, the action is more disruptive. (Opening an emergency exit door on an airplane qualifies.) The problem with "snapping" is that while it provides a momentary release of tension, it often comes with long-term consequences, such as getting fired, being formally disciplined, damaging your credibility with colleagues or direct reports, or losing an important client. And of course, in extreme examples, it can lead to violence.

Typically, the more that a difficult or negative emotion is routinely suppressed, the more likely it is that that emotion will erupt explosively. So, the question arises: why are we suppressing our emotions at work?

INTO THE CREVASSE

We may believe that expressing our feelings in some contexts is a virtue, and we may be vulnerable or lose our cool from time to time at home or with friends, but most of us long ago got the memo that unfiltered emotional reactivity is a big no-no at work. We don't need research to tell us not to scream at our boss, walk out of a team meeting in disgust, go mute with anxiety in the middle of a presentation, or cry anywhere outside a locked bathroom stall.

In the workplace, where freaking out isn't a viable option, emotional suppression is the number one barrier between us and our purpose. We equate professionalism and leadership with emotional suppression, and we don't see a problem with that (other than that it can be a challenge to maintain our composure on a particularly stressful day). We believe that productivity, professionalism, and respect are dependent upon our projecting an air of emotional neutrality and that it's on us to hide or deny our feelings at work. Thinking the feelings themselves are the problem, we try to get rid of them or ignore them altogether, not realizing how much of our mental resources are burned up in the effort. And the effort is a fruitless one. We think that stuffing our feelings down is the best and only way to get by at work, but when we do that, we block the pathway to a vital source of information: our emotions.

James Gross,[3] the godfather of the psychology of emotions and a senior professor at Stanford, was a pioneer in the field of emotion regulation before it was a field. His research has demonstrated very clearly that the more we try to get around our emotions, the worse off we are. Avoidance, rumination, and suppression all correlate with more anxiety and depression, negative emotions, less working memory, more stress, diminished feelings of authenticity, and a worsened ability to take tests. People who employ suppressive strategies to deal with their feelings are also seen as less likable by others.

There's a reason our emotions hang on so stubbornly despite our repeated attempts to extinguish or ignore them: we need them for our survival. We are hardwired as emotional creatures. Throughout the millennia of our evolution as social beings, feelings have been encoded into our DNA. They aren't an add-on but, rather, a key part of our makeup as humans. We are social creatures and have an incredible capacity to internalize social norms (how our actions will be interpreted by others). In our own emotional reactions, we can get quick and efficient information about what will fly with the members of our tribe (or office team). Our ability to register the group's norms efficiently in our own experience is the benefit that our interior, emotional lives offers us. According to Gross, the primary reason emotions exist is to prompt us to action. We can think of our emotions as alarm bells that alert us to pay attention to the things that are important to us. Our emotional response system is a biologically based, highly evolved mechanism of gathering information about our environment. This information allows us to see more clearly our goals and needs in a given situation.

For example, difficult emotions, such as anger or jealousy, are signals that we care about something. It's like the cliché goes: we don't pick a fight with someone we don't care about. The same principle applies when we feel irrationally upset with someone at work. When a coworker is driving us crazy, we can choose to take the perspective that we are upset because we care about our work. This is a good thing.

When we learn how to listen to our emotions, we can see that they are not a problem we need to fix. Rather, they are our very deepest source of wisdom. Listening to them is a survival skill. To turn them off is antithetical to our ability to function. In fact, one of the telltale signs of burnout is growing detached and cynical in our work relationships and duties.

To be clear, I'm not suggesting that we walk around the office letting everyone know how we feel about our day, about our boss, or about the organizations for which we work. But I would like to suggest that instead of ignoring or suppressing our feelings at work, we pay attention to them. The path to our purpose goes *through* our emotions—even (especially) the hard ones. In Buddhist tradition, we might use the metaphor of the snake trapped in a stalk of bamboo: There is no "getting around" our emotions. The only way out is through. If, say, a coworker is using humor that is making us uncomfortable, we might do well not to ignore that feeling. To do so is not only damaging to us but may also prove harmful to others.

Emotions at Work: The Gender Gap

When emotions appear to get in our way, it offers us an interesting opportunity to investigate what emotions are. According to a Kreamer Survey of two hundred[4] working Americans, women reported that they felt anger at work slightly more than men—51 percent versus 42 percent. But young men (42 percent) versus women (23 percent) believe that anger is an effective management tool. Forty-one percent of women reported that they had cried during the past year versus 9 percent of men. But here's one thing both sexes agreed on: 80 percent of the men and women surveyed said they would like to see more emotion expressed openly in the workplace.

What Doesn't Work

Given what we know from the research, we need to question the idea that we basically live in the upper few inches of our heads, and that emotions are add-ons that "happen" to us. Mindfulness offers us the tools for decoding our emotions and making it through to the other side of even the most difficult ones. When we cultivate self-awareness, we can learn our triggers and understand how to self-regulate or adapt to challenging situations. With self-compassion, we can experience an emotion without *becoming* it or acting on it in a way we'll regret. By setting intentions and working with our big-picture puzzle box cover in mind, we can listen to the wisdom our emotions have to offer and make better decisions.

When we suppress our emotions, we are also clouding judgment, blunting our emotional IQ, and increasing stress. Unfortunately, the evolutionary perspective on emotions too often gets boiled down to the idea that our feelings, once helpful in the context of saber-toothed tigers and hard-to-come-by food, are no longer adaptive in the modern world. The corresponding advice amounts to dealing with our feelings as so many false alarms. True, our emotions don't always reflect objective reality, but nor should we go too far the other way and categorically ignore them. There can be wisdom in our feelings even today, cues for adaptive behavior if we're willing to look for them and learn from them.

SUPPRESSION (AKA "STUFFING IT")

Suppressing our feelings doesn't work. My meditation teacher would use the metaphor of a balloon. We're the balloon, and if we suppress our emotions on one side, they are going to stick out somewhere else—and pop the balloon.

» Suppression Saps Our Energy

As James Gross explains, executive control is "the ability to inhibit a dominant response so as to activate a subdominant response." In plain English, that means going with a response other than the one we are most in the habit of going with. Without the ability to choose our response, we won't get very far toward our higher and longer-term goals. Also, if you are like me, you'll be too distracted by cookies and ice cream along the way. However, it takes effort to hold a poker face, grit our teeth, keep a stiff upper lip, and otherwise maintain executive control, especially if we're really upset. The anterior cingulate cortex, anterior insula, and basal ganglia in our brain can do only so much! Shutting out our less pleasant feelings so we don't have to feel them promotes a vicious circle, because those feelings don't actually go away. We have to white-knuckle it day in and day out to keep them suppressed, while we do nothing else about them. So the feelings remain, and the effort continues. This is energy we could be using for other things, such as pursuing our purpose or at least getting things done effectively. And with all this suppression-related energy expenditure, we're left with the feeling of barely staying afloat when we could be swimming.

» Suppression Backfires

Most of us have the goal of feeling good and moving toward a larger purpose, but emotions such as fear, anger, sadness, and jealousy can make us feel that our progress is backsliding. It's logical that we would focus on getting rid of these unpleasant feelings. The paradox that we run into is that this just doesn't work. The research consensus is that fighting against our feelings only makes them stronger. Trying to wrestle a negative affective state to the mat excites more activity in the amygdala. Our brains read this as more emotion and therefore spin faster and faster, until it becomes a vicious cycle and the whole dynamic is intensified. The ability to tolerate or accept or get curious about our unpleasant emotions is the ticket out of this cycle.

Emotions exist in the first place, according to psychologists, because they are supposed to prompt behavior. We exist in a social context, in an environment, and emotions are a quick way of getting feedback about how we are doing in relation to our environment. Evolutionarily speaking, they are designed to support us in safety. If we could shut them down to feel better, we wouldn't be very safe. If we remember that emotions are meant to help us negotiate our environment better, not necessarily to feel good all the time, we would see them differently. Then we could accept them rather than try to shut them off. We can and should use emotions to our benefit, as we do stress: when we see it as adaptive for our body, it becomes a way of getting important information that precipitates helpful reactions.

And just as stress is bad for our bodies, suppressing our emotions is, too. For example, if I'm angry at a coworker for interrupting me in midsentence, but I try to stuff down my anger, it will just flare up more. I might make it through the meeting, but the next time that coworker (or my parent/partner/friend/child) does something irritating, I'll blow my lid. As with that balloon we poke in, it inevitably pokes out on the other side.

» Suppression Is Bad for Our Health

Genomes (our complete set of DNA that holds all the information we need to function) exist fundamentally to help us succeed as humans. Insofar as this requires regulating our emotional experience (e.g., making compromises for the benefit of the tribe even when we don't feel like it, or not killing our children when they're being infuriating), the human genome must carry molecular blueprints to help us do this. Suppressing our emotions goes against these blueprints, and our long-term vitality pays the price. Studies conducted on the connection between emotion suppression and mortality risk show that suppressing one's emotions may create risk for earlier death, including from cancer. Further work is needed to better understand the biopsychosocial mechanisms for this risk and the nature of associations between suppression and different forms of mortality.

How we manage positive and negative emotions also plays a role in our maintaining cardiovascular health or developing cardiovascular disease, respectively. Suppressing our emotions requires psychological and physiological exertion—essentially a form of stress, leading to general wear and tear and increased vulnerability to disease over time. Conversely, studies have found that alternative, awareness-based strategies for dealing with our feelings reduce the risk of cardiovascular disease, and that the negative emotions themselves don't affect it one way or another. In other words, if we can regulate our emotions not by stuffing them down but by being aware of what they are, while they are happening, we can have the feeling but not *be had* by the feeling.

» Suppression Hurts Professional Relationships

Our relationships with our coworkers are the most valuable resource we have at our jobs. With our supervisors, supervisees, and peers, good relationships contribute to our productivity and enjoyment at work. Suppression damages relationships in three major ways. One is that we are perceived as inauthentic, which other people tend to take personally, thanks to the fundamental attribution error (i.e., the tendency to explain someone else's behavior based on internal rather than external factors). Second, suppression requires that we constantly edit ourselves when we interact with others. Every conversation therefore becomes a minefield that threatens to blow our cover, and every effort we make to guard ourselves is energy we don't have for solving other problems and doing our work. Finally, we can't relate to others' ups and downs without acknowledging our own, so suppression leaves us socially isolated and stuck in a holding pattern of small talk—what else is left to talk about?

» Suppression Hurts Our Personal Relationships

Suppression also denies us the full pleasure of close relationships, cutting us off from others—our coworkers, as already noted, but everyone else as well. When people have hostile experiences at work, they're more likely to be angry or withdrawn when they get home.

» Suppression Denies Us Good Feelings

Suppression is a crude strategy, like driftnet fishing. In the effort to target certain negative emotions, suppression ends up catching everything in its path. So we stuff down not only the unwanted emotions, but also our access to feelings we do want, such as joy, warmth, affection, and connections to others.

When we don't care, we don't feel. But if we are invested in our work, we will have feelings about not only the work but all things related to it. This is a sign of engagement. When we see something we judge as relevant to one of our goals, our emotion-processing networks address three basic questions: Is it good for me? Is it bad for me? What shall I do about it? So, if there's a conversation about a topic we care about during a meeting, we are more emotionally reactive. We are on heightened alert as to who is saying what, and our emotions are one of our most important tools for gathering important data.

The problem is that our emotions can, as the popular evolutionary theory goes, be maladaptive and lead to maladaptive behavior. We can misinterpret a situation, reading meaning into someone else's behavior that isn't there or carrying over an emotion from a previous exchange. For example, misreading the tone in an e-mail, which is so easy to do, or taking into your next meeting a disagreement you've just had on a phone call. To use the information offered to us by our emotions to our advantage, we need somehow to intervene between the emotion we experience and the behavior with which we instinctively respond. That's where mindfulness comes in.

In 2014, Bill Gross[5] (no relation to James Gross), then the bond manager at Pacific Investment Management Co., made headlines when he lashed out at two of his colleagues who had spoken to the press about his alleged abusive conduct. They described him as erratic, authoritarian, and prone to explosive tantrums. After this portrait appeared, Gross tried to have them fired. Instead, he claims in a lawsuit, *he* was fired. Now he is suing them for $200 million in damages.[6]

Gross is not the first high-powered executive to let stress make him lose his cool. *Harvard Business Review* has profiled film director James Cameron's harsh treatment of employees. Charlie Ergen's Dish Network was called by 24/7 Wall St. the "worst company to work for" and his behavior has been described as "publicly berating." Stanford researchers have studied such "scoundrels in the c-suite" to understand how boards should respond to CEO bad behavior most effectively (meaning it is a big enough problem that it warrants systematic study).

Mindfulness lets us "do" emotions differently. With mindfulness, we can, for example, recognize the emotion of anger before it's too late and we've done or said something regrettable. Mindfulness gives us a pause between feeling and action. In that little window, we have the opportunity to override the part of our evolutionary legacy that isn't appropriate to modern life and consciously adapt better responses. We can acknowledge the anger we feel, recognize its potential risks and benefits in a given situation, understand the information it offers us, and use that information to act in a way that is in accordance with our higher purpose. We can, for example, use the information of anger to recognize that we're being mistreated and channel that energy into becoming more assertive in sticking up for ourselves. If we are rubbed the wrong way by how a coworker is being treated, we can take that "energy" as the impetus to take a compassionate stand. Or if we recognize we are overcome by emotion, we might wait for it to dissipate first before we act.

With practice, we can become familiar with our usual patterns of emotional reactivity—remember, the English translation of the Tibetan word for "meditation" is "familiarization," as repeated contemplative practice makes us familiar with ourselves. When we are paying attention, we can notice clues, or what I call "emotional tells," which (again, if we are paying attention) tip us off to a potential threat or reaction *before* it happens, so we can become more intentional in the way we respond. These tells give us an advantage at work just as they do in poker. For example, we can notice anger building as we read a disparaging e-mail from a colleague who has cc'd the whole team. The earlier we notice our emotional reaction, the more we are able to pause before we respond. If we wait too long, our emotions can become overwhelming or completely hijack our mood, calcifying emotions into judgments and beliefs about our situation. Early detection buys us time to make choices about our emotions—how to interpret them, whether and how to act on them. Paying attention to emotional tells also gives us insight into the environment and people around us that we can use for decision making and determining action.

In his book *Thinking, Fast and Slow*,[7] the Nobel Prize–winning economist Daniel Kahneman tells the story of an experienced firefighter who ordered his crew out of a burning building just before it collapsed. When asked how he knew that danger was imminent, he traced his decision back to the sensation of heat on his ears. He paid attention to a subtle feeling that experience and familiarization had taught him was a tell for danger. We, too, can build a base of knowledge by becoming experienced with the situations that trigger us and familiar with the physical sensations, thoughts, and emotional impulses that signal danger. We can parlay this information into more accurate, fast judgments. Mindfulness of our emotions lets us feel the emotional equivalent of heat on our ears, and do something about it. Kahneman's phrase "intuition is recognition" neatly sums up what so many people who practice mindfulness report: namely, that subtler cues become available to them. These cues let us access our knowledge quickly and make us aware of multiple ways of knowing.

As mindfulness shows us, the idea of purely rational behavior (the core of traditional historical economic theory) is not a realistic one, according to myriad research on human behavior, which cites emotion, mood, and social input as key factors in decision making. This is an insight that mainstream economists have long acknowledged. Emotions play an important role in decision making, and our inability to account for this is one reason that models in economics fail to predict behavior in the real world so much of the time.

Emotions and Decision Making

Jonathan Haidt[8] is a social psychologist and professor of leadership at NYU's Stern School of Business, where his research is focused on morality, emotions, and decision making. Haidt's interest is in the context of moral decision making and the ways in which emotions influence ethical decisions. He says that our internalized versions of cultural norms, what he has coined as "social intuitionist" factors, can prompt us to make automatic, knee-jerk responses to moral questions. He describes such responses as "gut reactions of the mind." As humans, we use what Haidt calls "moral intuition" and then tend to justify these gut reactions with logical arguments after the fact. For example, we have a felt sense that a coworker's joke was out of bounds but we use a rationalization to explain this feeling.

Haidt's approach is not dissimilar to the "thin slicing" phenomenon that Malcolm Gladwell made popular in his bestselling book *Blink*, drawing on researchers such as Kenney, Malloy, and Thorndike. The upshot is that we believe we make decisions as rational individuals, but in fact, we make snap judgments, based on emotions that are internalized social and cultural norms. And the whole process is fast and largely unconscious.

Much of our behavior is driven by our emotions or our reactions to our emotions, even if it doesn't feel that way. As researchers such as Haidt have shown, our particular idiosyncrasies and histories inform our responses to our environment. Each of us sees the world in his or her own way and brings a specific belief system and underlying assumptions to any given situation. As a result, we often jump to conclusions and act based on those assumptions, which are not necessarily "objectively" correct. (We assume others view the world in the same way we do, too, but of course, that is also not the case.) This idea of interpreting the world around us according to our own experience is sometimes referred to as the "ladder of inference."

The Ladder of Inference

The ladder of inference is a process by which we jump from observation of data in the environment to interpretation of that data. Knowing this ladder exists can help us observe our own ladder-jumping reactions. Mindfulness lets us see how we are climbing this ladder of inference, in terms of the stories we tell ourselves and the emotions we experience. By being aware of each of these steps of taking in information from our environment—so-and-so says such-and-such, and we interpret him to be acting in a vindictive way toward us—we separate out what we observed from the inferences/stories we tell ourselves. And knowing what is driving our assumptions, conclusions, emotions, and actions is an important part of our being mindful. When we are able to see ourselves in action, to have awareness of the meta-moment, we can change our response before it's too late. When we pause to listen to the scripts in our heads, we can question whether those scripts are true. When we learn to identify our emotions, we can label which ones are truly wise and which might be a misleading by-product of the second arrow. Getting curious about where our ideas and feelings come from is the first step.

It's important to keep in mind that while our emotions happen in response to situations, situations don't create our emotional responses. It is the way we interpret or appraise a situation that creates our emotional response to it. This is where experience and judgment come into play. Focus is a useful tool when it comes to regulating our emotional responses. When we have the ability to shift our focus, we can then place our attention on observable data. Once we recognize that we are climbing the ladder of inference, we can descend back to less subjective information. For example, when a coworker says something that upsets us, we can ask a question that will help us parse what that person's motivation was. It could be as simple as asking him what he meant by the remark, or observing that he seems upset and trying to draw out further information from him.

Accomplish This:
Identify the Ladder of Inference

Paying attention and recognizing when we are climbing the ladder of inference can offer us the opportunity to shift our attention to objective data, rather than react to subjective feelings. Bring to mind a recent situation at work that caused you to experience difficult emotions and then try the following:

- Write down how the situation made you feel. What were your strongest emotions? Fear? Anxiety? Panic?
- Now take a moment to write or reflect on the facts of the situation. What actually happened?
- Next, take a step back. What would an objective observer say about the situation? Did what actually happened warrant the emotions you felt? Was the eventual outcome as terrible as you thought it was? Practice identifying what you are inferring through your emotional responses versus what is actually provable based on fact.

Mindfulness Strategies for Emotional Regulation

Many people think mindfulness means unfeelingness. They imagine that if they are good at mindfulness they will always be calm, won't feel anything too intensely, that mindfulness will clear their minds of all the heat and noise. But being mindful of your emotions doesn't mean not having emotions. Sadly, this misperception often prevents people from tapping into the wisdom of their emotions. If they knew the potential for insight and learning, they wouldn't want to get rid of their emotions even if they could. A major function of mindfulness is to help you see emotions for what they are: feedback on the world—no more, no less.

Anyone who starts the practice of mindfulness, who pays attention to her inner experience without using suppression, starts to notice a lot of stuff—and some of it is not pretty. Again, we are like the snake in the bamboo shoot. We see this stuff, and we can't go around it, as much as we wish we could. The only way out of the bamboo shoot is to go through it. People who are new to mindfulness practice often complain when they see the incredible amount of inner churn going on all the time. They think that their self-awareness practice created this churn. Usually, though, when they stay with it, they come to realize that the churn was already there; they were just avoiding seeing it, like a child with his fingers in his ears saying, "I can't hear you!" When we begin a mindfulness practice, we are able to see the damaging patterns, but we have yet to develop the strength to avoid being overwhelmed by them.

Emotion regulation gives us strategies to recognize and influence our relationship with our emotions, including what type they are and how much/how long/and how they play out in our behavior. So how does this work in action, in a professional setting? Here are a few effective strategies drawn from research and my own curriculum.

REFRAME/REAPPRAISE

We all have habits of interpretation of our emotions that don't serve us, but it's possible to rework them. The more self-aware you are about your emotions, the stronger your ability to do this effectively, which builds on the foundation of the mindfulness you are practicing.

Recognizing that the way you interpret any given situation is subjective means you can reappraise it and react in a healthier way. For example, if you are angry at your boss because he didn't give you the information you needed to do something successfully, you can be maladaptive, stomping around and complaining angrily, or you can be adaptive by knowing that it's up to you to get the feedback you need. Schedule a meeting with your boss and approach him when you're feeling rational.

ACCEPT

Having clarity regarding your emotions is the key to accepting them. This requires the ability to recognize them, name them, and understand them. Some of the phrases used in psychology to teach acceptance of emotions are: "catch yourself reacting," understand your "triggers," and (in business/leadership contexts) "know your tuning."

The next time you're experiencing a difficult situation at work, think about the bigger picture of your life and ask yourself whether this difficulty might be a part of a larger pattern. Do you have a tendency to avoid conflict? Do you start things and struggle to finish them? Do you place a lot of trust in people and feel disappointed when they don't perform up to your standards? Do you have expectations for yourself that you don't often meet? How do these patterns relate to your current situation and to the stories you've been paying attention to over the past week? When you become disproportionately upset by a small comment or beyond what is called for in a given situation, what do you think was the trigger? What "tells" do you notice when triggered?

When I was working with veterans at the Veterans Administration, I studied a system called ACT, or acceptance and commitment therapy. This practical application of emotional regulation is completely consistent with mindfulness practice. ACT focuses on three tasks:

1. Accept your reactions and be present.
2. Choose a valued direction.
3. Take action.[9]

The first step, acceptance, means not avoiding or suppressing our emotions. Next, choosing a valued direction gives us clarity on what matters to us and connects us with our purpose, allowing us to consider how it maps onto a particular situation. We then can act with our feelings clarified and our goals in mind.

ACT offers a five-step process for accepting emotions:

1. Let your feelings or thoughts happen without the impulse to act on them.
2. Observe your weaknesses but take note of your strengths.

3. Give yourself permission not to be good at everything.

4. Acknowledge the difficulty in your life without escaping from it or avoiding it.

5. Realize that you can be in control of how you react, think, and feel.

ACT also uses a concept called defusion, which helps us realize that thoughts and feelings are not factual truths carved in stone but, rather, sensations and reactions that will pass. There is also a saying in AA that expresses this idea: "feelings aren't facts." I like this idea of defusion; it makes me think of a bomb metaphor: if we don't recognize what we are feeling, then we are tick, tick, ticking away, ready to explode.

PROBLEM-SOLVE

When we face a recurring difficult situation every day, it can be a real drain on our mental and physical energies. Elisa Jagerson, the CEO of Speck Design, says she realized that her transition from work to home each day was not going well, particularly as it involved her young children. As soon as she walked in the door at the end of the day, her kids were all over her, and Elisa, already exhausted, felt overwhelmed and stressed out by their needs. She realized that the process of arriving home from a long day of work needed an overhaul. Simply changing out of her work clothes before she got home allowed her to relate to her kids more intentionally and happily. Instead of worrying about keeping their sticky hands off her business wardrobe, now she could be fully present, willing, and able to scoop them up and give them the attention they were craving.

Putting a physical ritual in place for ourselves when we arrive home, whether it's changing our clothes or docking our devices, completes the workday or at least signals a period of attention to home before resuming work activities if we have to do them later.

Accomplish This: Walking Meditation

Sometimes you might find yourself flooded with emotion and unable to take yourself calmly through the process of identifying and listening to your emotions. In moments such as these, one of the quickest ways to shift your focus is to rest your attention in the body. By returning your focus to your body, you can move your mind off thoughts of other things.

One way to do this is to go for a walk, or to practice what is known as "walking meditation." When you practice walking meditation, you just go for a stroll. According to Thich Nhat Hanh's definition,

> [Y]ou have no purpose or direction in space or time. The purpose of walking meditation is walking meditation itself. Going is important, not arriving. Walking meditation is not a means to an end; it is an end.
>
> Walking meditation is learning to walk again with ease. When you were about a year old, you began to walk with tottering steps. Now, in practicing walking meditation[,] you are learning to walk again.
>
> Put your attention on the soles of your feet and feel them making contact with the ground.
>
> Stand on one foot, and be aware that it is resting upon the earth. While walking, look down and anticipate the ground where you are about to place your foot, and when you do, mindfully experience your foot, the ground, and the connection between your foot and the ground.

Take a few more minutes to experiment with this. If it feels relaxing, great. If it feels absurd, great.

Knowing we are walking when we are walking—it sounds simple, but it is hard to do. As with breath meditation, our minds wander off. Walking meditation needs tailoring specifically to when our emotions are heightened. It might be that we keep our attention on the soles of our feet striking the ground to calm ourselves. Then we might pay attention to the part of the body where our emotions are showing up (e.g., our chest, abdomen), feeling the physical components of the emotion and focusing on those rather than the storyline that elicited those emotions in the first place and that tend to rev us up. While we are moving, we should feel the emotion as a direct, physical experience. This can be a short recentering exercise or something we do for longer if we can swing it.

You can apply the practice of walking meditation to your workouts, too—especially if they involve repetitive motions such as running, walking, cycling, or rowing.

Mindfulness and Candor: What's Your Worst Fear?

Becoming aware of fear is an excellent opportunity to see your scripts, the stories you're telling yourself. These scripts can get in the way of many things, primarily change. So, first you need to see that the fear of speaking up is just a story, then figure out what that story is, and finally tell yourself a different one.

Notice when you're holding back and ask yourself, "What is my worst fear?" Are you afraid of disagreement? Criticism? Afraid of stating the obvious? Afraid that your idea isn't good enough and everyone will see that you're a fraud? Afraid that if your idea is taken up, you'll be blamed for anything that goes wrong? Afraid you'll die of embarrassment? Often our worst unspoken fears are fundamentally outrageous, about things that are basically impossible (such as actually dying of embarrassment). In the middle of a meeting, we might notice our heart is racing, signaling to our brain that our life is on the line. If we take that short pause to check in with ourselves, we'll see that we're in full-blown fight-or-flight mode, but the reality is we are fairly unlikely to be beaten to death in the conference room. Seeing feelings as feelings (meaning as sensations in the body rather than as a reason to run screaming from the room) and stories as stories (rather than undeniable facts) gives us a choice to transform the moment of panic into one of self-compassion (I'm only human), connection (we're all human), and even humor ("My first flop sweat at my new job! It's a milestone!"). From that instant of authentic communication with ourselves, we can speak with candor, even if we are still feeling terrified (though this kind of checking in is like a steam valve: it generally brings the terror down dramatically).

PRACTICE DOING THE OPPOSITE

Sometimes our patterns of behavior are a way for us to avoid candor. If we are uncomfortable with confrontation, for example, we might hold our tongues but then speak about our frustration to a third party. Recognize this habit of communication and then try to do the opposite, or at least something slightly different.

Any interaction can be an opportunity for shaking things up through conscious participation. Do you tend to speak up first in meetings, or are you someone who doesn't speak at all or who waits until the end? Sometimes we believe that our habitual behavior is because "it's just who we are," but the way things tend to be isn't necessarily the way they have to be. Experiment with shifting your behavior. If you usually jump in first, what happens if you hold off and let others speak? This doesn't mean you should never speak, but do see what changes happen in the room if you aren't the first to do so. When we change our behavior, it can be like turning over a rock; we have to wait and see what comes out. You will learn a lot.

Alternatively, if you tend to hang back in meetings, see what happens if you speak up sooner. Think of it as an experiment: ask a question or make a small observation and see how that action impacts your experience of the moment and of the overall exchange. Other habits you may notice could include interrupting, phrasing ideas as questions rather than assertions, or engaging in the currently controversial "vocal fry." In fact, just noticing or being mindful of our habits can change them. According to the Pew Research Center,[10] 69 percent of American adults keep track of at least one health indicator such as weight, diet, exercise, or a bodily symptom, and the act of tracking it (on paper or with a device) impacts the behavior associated with the data being tracked. The same principle holds true when it comes to our habits in the workplace.

PLAN YOUR REACTION

Especially if you are someone who often experiences emotional flooding or anxiety, it's helpful to give yourself a script so that, in the moment, you can respond as you intended instead of reacting from your lizard brain. Nonverbal grounding techniques such as feeling the ground beneath your feet or your chair under you, allowing yourself to feel literally supported by these solid things, can have a similar effect. When you are triggered (upset or up-regulated), it has an observable impact on your body, behavior, and interactions. Learning when, how, and why you are triggered, becoming more familiar with your inner experience and your "tells," will increase your capacity to steward your behavior. Think of the last time you were triggered at work. What was the context? What did that feel like? What did you do?

Anticipate the next stressful event you are likely to encounter and try to see it as an opportunity to learn more about your triggers. Come up with healthy alternative responses. When you find yourself being triggered, stay attuned to those sensations and recognize that your logic and rationality are impaired at the moment. It is the time not to do anything rash or reactive but, rather, to focus your attention on what you are feeling and how you are experiencing the situation and to wait until you are calmed down before you do anything major.

REFRAME: THE OTHER IS NOT THE ENEMY

The other is not even "other," really. From the perspective of compassion, the person you're negotiating with, or fighting with (actually or in your head), or who is just plain driving you crazy in the moment or in an ongoing way—that person is a being just like you, someone who has a life and hopes and dreams and fears. Think about him in other roles or at other times in his life. Think of him as a child whom someone cared for, fed, and taught to read and tie his shoes. Think of him being a parent, a partner, or helping his aging parents. Keep in mind that just as you are wrestling with doing your best with your history and demons, so is he. He is not the enemy.

Making enemies of others is typically an attribution error because most of if not all human behavior is dependent on a person's circumstances, and in the case of our colleagues and others at work, we are not usually privy to those circumstances. As David Foster Wallace articulated it in his now-famous commencement speech at Kenyon College,[11] "Most days, if you're aware enough to give yourself a choice, you can choose to look differently at this fat, dead-eyed, over-made-up lady who just screamed at her kid in the checkout line. Maybe she's not usually like this. Maybe she's been up three straight nights holding the hand of a husband who is dying of bone cancer. Or maybe this very lady is the low-wage clerk at the Motor Vehicle department, who just yesterday helped your spouse resolve a horrific, infuriating, red-tape problem through some small act of bureaucratic kindness."

A graphic designer I know calls this kind of thinking "perspectiflex." Choosing to appraise a situation differently, and with compassion, rather than taking a blaming, damning approach, is the way out of the war. Fake-it-till-you-make-it applies here, too: buy a cup of coffee for the person you think you can't stand, compliment his shoes, act "as if" you not only can stand him but actually care for him.

REMEMBER THAT WORK ISN'T EVERYTHING

If the worst is possible and does happen—if you are shamed, ridiculed, fired—remembering your larger purpose will put work into a more manageable perspective. This is one reason it's so important to hone our sense of purpose when we're not in crisis, because it will be critical to our resilience when we are.

A study[12] of people who lost their jobs in the 2004 economic downturn showed a direct relationship between a multifaceted sense of purpose (including many different relationships, values, and roles) and the ability to bounce back. In a traditional Tibetan reflection, we contemplate the preciousness of our lives and all we can do with them, and the inevitability of suffering. This is the big picture, and we can practice calling it up at any time. As Guru Rinpoche puts it, we want to have a view as high as the sky and attention as meticulous as finely ground barley flour. So, while we attend to everything at work with care, we also know what matters beyond it.

Accomplish This: Quick Ways to Access Mindfulness at Work

- Practice tracking and tweaking your habitual routines; you may experience new outcomes as a result.
- Take ideas at face value: separate them from the person sharing them.
- Before going into situations that are likely to provoke anxiety, give yourself a script to fall back on if unpleasant emotions arise.

- Ask yourself, "What's my worst fear?" Identify the barriers you have to speaking with candor.
- Take a meditation walk before work or on your lunch break.
- Pay attention to your body language; understand the meaning that certain gestures or behaviors may convey.
- Reframe any perceived enemies for what they are: humans, just like you, making their way through the world.
- Practice being happy for other people's good fortune.
- When feeling marginalized, take action to engage and participate rather than sinking into feelings of inadequacy or isolating yourself.
- Put work into perspective: it isn't everything.
- Have real check-ins with others about how you, and they, are doing.

Even if you follow every piece of advice I offer in this chapter, you won't wake up tomorrow to a workday devoid of new challenges, or succeed in accepting every difficult emotion that surfaces in response to those challenges. And that's okay. But you can start the day by setting the intention to feel your emotions and not react. And then, tomorrow, one of your coworkers will piss you off. And you will react. And, later, you will remember that you meant to accept your feelings and not bite that person's head off. And that will be okay, too.

Remember, just as having emotions is not a failure, reacting to emotions is not the end of the world, either. Stuffing them down—well, it happens sometimes. On our journey, there will be gaps between who we intend to be and who we are. The failure is in not minding these gaps. This is where our best growth potential lies.

Part III

FAILING AND REFLECTING

The Traits of Successful People and Organizations

7

Fail Better

How Reflection Helps Us Learn and Grow

EVER TRIED. EVER FAILED. NO MATTER. TRY AGAIN. FAIL AGAIN. FAIL
BETTER.

—"Worstward Ho," Samuel Beckett

At some point in recent history, this bleak and somewhat obscure line from existentialist playwright Samuel Beckett became the motto of the new entrepreneurialism. It isn't clear if it was business mogul Richard Branson, self-help author Timothy Ferriss, tennis pro Stanislas Wawrinka (who has "Fail Better" tattooed on his arm), or someone else who first adopted the term, but somewhere along the line the business crowd embraced it. Perhaps because "failure" sounds grander than "mistake." Perhaps because so many start-ups that failed out of the gate went on to become household names. In any event, this Beckett prose piece became a popular catchphrase, first in the tech world and now in just about every sector.

People have always made mistakes and sometimes tried to learn from them, but the entrepreneurial embrace of the "fail better" philosophy suddenly put defeat on a pedestal, making it a cause for celebration.

An abundance of anecdotes and examples was found to affirm this ethos: Winston Churchill failed the sixth grade. Ben Franklin's inventions didn't always work. Early in her career as a television reporter, Oprah Winfrey was fired. History is full of persevering heroes who failed on the way to success.

In a recent article he posted to LinkedIn,[1] Microsoft cofounder Paul Allen wrote that Microsoft might not exist if he and Bill Gates hadn't failed with their first company (a traffic data–analyzing project called, naturally, Traf-O-Data). "While Traf-O-Data was technically a *business failure*," Allen wrote, "the understanding of microprocessors we absorbed was crucial to our *future* success. And the emulator I wrote to program it gave us a huge head start over anyone else writing code at the time. If it hadn't been for our Traf-O-Data venture, and if it hadn't been for all that time spent on UW computers, you could argue that Microsoft might not have happened. I hope the lesson is that there are few true dead ends in computer science. Sometimes taking a step in one direction positions you to push ahead in another one."

As "fail better" achieved meme status in Silicon Valley, where it captured the spirit of the aggressive optimism and "disruptive" thinking beloved by start-up business culture, the irony of the expression's original and famously pessimistic coiner, Samuel Beckett, was lost on most. In the backlash, however, some nonliterary critics dismissed "fail better" as wishful or even reckless thinking. Mindfulness acknowledges both these points of view. From a Buddhist perspective, "failing better" means acknowledging human imperfection and accepting that failure is part of the learning process—if we give people room to learn. Failing better means trying and trying again, but with a difference. Reflection makes the difference, and not just in Silicon Valley.

Harvard Business School professor Francesca Gino[2] has researched the role of reflection in the workplace and found that it is worth the time not only in the wisdom it generates but also in the productivity that emerges. One of her studies, which she conducted at the IT firm

Wipro in Bangalore, India, examined how providing structure for reflection and for sharing about work impacted follow-up on various tasks. The researchers studied several groups of employees in their initial weeks of training for a particular customer account and divided them into three groups: the control group, the reflection group, and the sharing group.

In the reflection group, on the sixth through the sixteenth days of training, workers spent the last fifteen minutes of each day writing and reflecting on the lessons they had learned that day. Participants in the sharing group did the same, but spent an additional five minutes explaining their notes to a fellow trainee. Those in the control group just kept working at the end of the day and did not receive additional training.

Over the course of one month, workers in both the reflection and sharing groups performed significantly better than those in the control group. On average, the reflection group increased its performance on the final training test by 22.8 percent as compared to the control group. The sharing group performed 25 percent better on the test than the control group, about the same increase as for the reflection group. In addition, the participants who had been put in the reflection group (rather than the practice group) "improved their likelihood of being in the top-rated category of all trainees by 19.1%." The same researchers also studied whether people appreciate the power of reflection, and they learned that when given the choice, 210 out of 256 participants opted to get more experience and only 18 percent chose to have reflection time. Reflection is clearly valuable but it isn't necessarily valued.

Just like pausing before we jump into something (which is what we do when we set our intentions), pausing *after* we have jumped into something takes only a moment, but has a profound impact. We pause not to slow down, necessarily, but to reperceive our thoughts, emotions, and context with fresh perspective. Practice makes perfect, perhaps, but in practice we also see how far from perfect we are.

Similarly, when we try to be more compassionate, toward others or our-selves, we also notice how we're not; and when we care about suffering in the workplace, we realize that we often don't know how to make things better. It's like the physical assessment you have with a trainer when you first join a gym, testing your body to see where it is weak, as part of the process of building strength. Physical, emotional, and mental learning all depend on nonjudgmental pauses for realistic self-appraisal, re-mindfulness of our intentions, and rededication to our purpose. Sometimes what we see in these moments isn't what we'd hoped for. But instead of viewing our failures as evidence that we suck at our jobs or that we are worthless as people, we can choose to ap-proach them as evidence that we are engaging, that we are working at it, and that we will get there.

With all the talk of embracing failure, there is less talk in corpo-rate culture of reflection, but that's just what Severin Schwan, CEO of biotech giant Roche, touched on in a 2014 interview with Reuters[3] entitled "For Roche's CEO, Celebrating Failure Is the Key to Success." In the piece, he emphasizes the need to foster acceptance of failure as a necessary part of innovation. "We need a culture where people take risks[,] because if you don't take risks, you won't have breakthrough innovation," he said. But he also went on to suggest that it's important for managers to praise people for the nine times they fail, not just the one time they succeed. Schwan even takes his direct reports out to lunch to celebrate their failures. Rituals like this offer an opportunity for reflection.

The person who encouraged me to attend my first-ever meditation retreat, a mentor I had known since childhood, told me that transi-tions were the times of the day to pay the most attention to, for ex-ample, when you are moving from morning to afternoon, from one project to another, or from work to home. She told me not to think of the cushion part of meditation as the main event but, instead, to notice the thoughts and habits that come up when we're *not* meditating. When we pay attention to the transitions, the spaces in between become their own instruction.*

What Is Reflection?

The idea of reflection is not a new one. Many thousands of years ago, Socrates said that "the unexamined life is not worth living." Philosophers have long argued that the capacity for self-reflection is what sets us apart as humans. Reflection is an ancient practice that has been embraced by psychology, education, leadership development, and the wisdom traditions for a common reason: because it works.

When we are busy with our lives and constantly exposed to the promise of sexy new information, things, and experiences, it seems impossible to take this time to fully experience what is happening and to then process it. But taking a step back to reflect allows us to see our experiences, our behavior, and the behavior of others from a different perspective. Nonetheless, reflection often gets a bad rap as passive, open ended, and divorced from a results-oriented approach.

The word *reflection* has two meanings that, at first glance, may appear unrelated. The first is "the throwing back by a body or surface of light, heat, or sound without absorbing it." The second is "serious thought or consideration." As you can see, the first definition is actually very useful in terms of understanding the second. The mirroring-back part of reflection implies that we can recognize the overlay that our stories, fears, and projections cast on events so that we can see the events more clearly and respond more skillfully. This is an important point because when reflection turns into musings that do not accurately

---

* Further reading on "transitional prompts": www.leahweissphd.com/transitional-prompts.

reflect what is happening, it isn't useful. We need to be judicious about knowing when we are adding layers and be open to these layers being off base. Reflection has a relationship to what actually happens. With reflection, we can create a stronger relationship to our experience than our usual partial, biased, semiconscious one. When we consider something deeply, and with precision, we see it more clearly.

One of my Buddhist teachers, Charles Genoud, uses the term *intimacy* for this idea of becoming more familiar with our experience by paying close and precise attention to it without adulterating it with our ideas. Reflection allows us to become intimate with our own way of thinking and doing and being. If we don't take the time to reflect, we can't learn anything or absorb new information, but many of us actually don't know how to reflect. We haven't learned how, or it isn't a part of our workflow.

In the context of getting work done, this intimacy is about the distinction between data and interpretation. We typically see what we expect to see, so this is harder than it sounds. For example, if a coworker interrupts us in an important meeting, it might trigger us to go on the offensive. We assume that the colleague is trying to silence us when in fact she may just be distracted (not malicious), or exhausted from staying up the night before with a sick child. Instead of getting angry, consider the other possibilities for the interruption.

Accomplish This:
Change Your Interpretation

Sometimes when we're faced with a challenging situation, we assume the worst. That we blew a big presentation, that we will never make a deadline, that we made a mistake that has surely jeopardized our job security. The next time you find yourself feeling this way, consider that your interpretation of the problem at hand may not be accurate. I suggest trying a quick experiment designed to challenge your perception.

Find a piece of paper and a pen. On one side of the paper, report what happened or is happening—just the facts as you know them (example: my boss coughed during my presentation). On the other side, write down what meaning you made of it (example: she was signaling that I am not a good presenter and more specifically that I should wrap it up so the group could get on to the discussion). Look at the situation itself and then reflect on your interpretation of it. Is there any way that different interpretations of the issue might also be valid (example: it is cold and flu season)? Write those down, too. Now consider all the ways this event might be interpreted (example: maybe she wasn't coughing because I'm a bad presenter, maybe she was coughing because she is sick or has allergies). Are you still sure your interpretation is correct?

Silence, introspection, articulation, and feedback are all part of the process of reflection. Reflection can be practiced in many different ways: quiet thinking, meditation, talking with others, listening to others, listening to oneself, praying, learning, or just being.

Each of the wisdom traditions includes rituals around reflection. For example, in Judaism, Yom Kippur is a day earmarked for reflecting on the prior year, which sets you up for making intentional choices for the coming year, meaning that we can then start the new year with the benefit of insight drawn from reflection. In Christianity, prayer and retreat are seen as opportunities to reflect on our actions and behavior. Muslim prayer intersperses these moments of reflection throughout the day. Quakers gather together and sit in silence in order to reflect.

Boston College theologian Colleen Griffith, a mentor of mine, is an expert in Christian spirituality. In her research, writing, and teaching, she helps people unpack traditional interpretations of Christian doctrine, making them relevant today in order to enrich people's lives and strengthen their faith. One of the topics she addresses is the notion of reflection with religious images. Images, she suggests, can help people tap into their authentic values and allow them to transcend the materialistic concerns that so readily grab their attention. The process of reflection that she describes involves slowing down, spending time with an image that calls to you (perhaps a beautiful place you once visited), dropping prior conceptions of the image, and seeing what the image evokes.

From a Buddhist perspective, reflection is a way to choose to reframe our understanding, by practicing again and again when thoughts come up that get in the way of our goals. In *The Art of Happiness at Work*,[4] the Dalai Lama suggests many ways we can practice reflection in the workplace. He discusses the importance of making an effort to strive toward finding and doing our best work. He also says that "if that fails, then instead of frustration, or becoming angry focusing only on the thought, *I tried but I wasn't able to make it*—then think, *O.K., I'll carry on with this work*." He tells us to be content with the work we have and reframe a bad situation. This type of reflection is paramount in the mind-training tradition. Mind training can eliminate anger and frustration and foster a better attitude. We have more agency in shaping our experience than we realize. Our habits of interpretation keep us in the same habits of experience. It's like *Groundhog Day*: we experience the same thing over and over. So, even though it will feel artificial at first and until you get good at it, instead of being stuck in a habit of reaction and action, experiment with a new thought. Ask a question that gets at the opposite of your assumption: Is it true? In terms of the *dampa sum* ("good in the beginning, good in the middle, good in the end"), reflection is understood to be the difference between having practice make you feel temporarily better (more relaxed, for example) or having it lead to transformation (understood as enlightenment in the Buddhist worldview).

Like rituals, slogans can also remind us to unpack our assumptions. For example, "Is this true?" or "Next time do the opposite/don't be so predictable" can help us identify when we've gotten stuck in an unhelpful way of thinking, often without noticing it and out of habit. I have inherited the strong tendency to kvetch about this and that, so practicing the slogan "Don't bring things to a painful point" was immensely helpful in my early training, to help me catch myself when I was complaining or being disparaging. Such a slogan doesn't mean we can't reflect on a situation and offer critical feedback, but it can make us aware of the knee-jerk habit of complaining and creating downer interactions that serve no greater purpose.

From a psychological point of view, cognitive behavioral therapy (CBT)—a highly effective form of psychotherapy first developed by the American psychologist Aaron Beck in the 1960s—includes extensive reflection techniques. CBT has been used successfully to treat patients with diverse mental health issues, from depression to schizophrenia, and those with cancer, diabetes, cardiac issues, and migraines.

Essentially, CBT is a problem-solving approach in which the person in treatment investigates the impact of his thoughts by being systematically walked through the process of unpacking habitual responses. This type of reflection allows us to experiment with our behavior to test how we can intervene in our own loops of reaction-action-interpretation. More recently, mindfulness-based therapies (mindfulness-based cognitive therapy, acceptance therapy, commitment therapy, and dialectical behavioral therapy) have also gained popularity.

Reflecting on automatic thoughts and habitual behaviors is key to all these techniques. If a colleague gives you feedback about how you perform a task, and your automatic thought is that he is implicitly criticizing your past performance or suggesting you are incompetent or that he is better than you, these techniques can help you work through such thoughts. You pick the thought that is causing you the pain and literally write out evidence in support of its being true or not. By examining our assumptions and thoughts, we gain perspective. This type of authentic reflection allows us to learn and grow. So, the next time someone interrupts you in a meeting, try to rethink the meaning of the event. Challenge yourself to access your curiosity, perhaps asking a question about the question or thought that to this person feels pressed to express.

Reflection is regarded as a fundamental part of effective education as well. In his 1934 book *Art as Experience*, John Dewey, perhaps the most impactful educator of the twentieth century, writes that we have experiences literally all the time but don't necessarily learn from them. Dewey saw reflection as crucial to education because many of us can grow old without becoming wise. Experience itself does not guarantee anything.

Dewey's philosophy was a reversal of the accepted model of teaching, which was based on the traditional hierarchy of teacher and student in which the teacher gives information and the student simply memorizes it. Dewey rejected this rote learning and believed that what people learned should matter to them, to their lives. He suggested that the fit between the content and the learner was a vital piece of the puzzle, and argued for learning by doing (rather than listening and memorizing).

Dewey felt also that the traditional education model was overly focused on preparing for the future and neglected to recognize the importance of the present. He believed that experiencing the present was the best preparation for the future—which sounds a lot like a Buddhist perspective. Dewey embedded the idea of reflection into this idea of fully experiencing the present. The notion of extracting the full meaning of the present experience, which he argued was indispensable to education, is precisely the process of reflection. Reflection is the way we learn cause and effect and how to anticipate consequences and select future actions.

Reflection is an important part of the workday for everyone, and that includes those at the top. Developing a learning or growth mind-set is a crucial skill for leaders. Psychologist and author of *Mindset*, Carol Dweck,[5] has researched and written extensively about motivation and what it takes to foster a growth mind-set. She suggests that people adopt in the workplace either a performance or a learning mind-set. A performance mind-set is one that focuses on achievement and proving your value. In this context, looking good, appearing smarter than others, or cultivating a mirage of perfection are the goals. A learning mind-set, on the other hand, allows for everyone to change and grow through experience. It offers a context in which we can learn from our mistakes and therefore become more innovative and open to taking risks. Instead of being motivated by fear or becoming paralyzed by it, we can move outside our comfort zones and push our boundaries, gaining strength, resilience, and new skills in the process.

With organizations spending upwards of $70 billion in the United States alone (and $130 billion globally) on employee training, it is important to know which types of training are the most useful. Research suggests that providing workers with built-in contexts (readings, research, documents that pertain to a particular topic) to reflect on, summarize, and express what they are doing and learning is a more effective training strategy than simply adding more experiences without the chance to reflect on them. While it's true that this can be uncomfortable or counterintuitive for some—most of us seem to prefer *doing* things rather than *reflecting* on things—reflection, not action, is what leads to improved performance.

What does reflection look like in the context of work? Basically, it means creating a system or workflow that allows employees the opportunity to reflect on experiences and learn from them. When we get caught up in the next task, we don't necessarily learn from our experiences. The Michigan Model of Leadership, out of the University of Michigan's Ross School of Business, is understood to be "an active process of probing cause-and-effect, questioning assumptions, and analyzing the meaning of experience." The Ross School has developed a process called an "after-action review." After an event, people walk through what actually occurred and look at the data rather than the attributions we make when we climb the ladder of inference without realizing we are doing it. This can be done alone, through peer coaching, or in a team discussion.

Research[6] has shown that this process of after-action review results in an 8 percent increase in leadership effectiveness ratings, a 9 percent increase in job offers, and a 10 percent increase in starting salaries for individuals. The process hinges on committing to a learning mind-set, experimenting, seeking feedback, paying attention to emotions, and then reflecting to absorb lessons from the experience. With a learning mind-set, we can see ourselves as able to change and grow in our reactions to workplace situations. For example, instead of butting heads with a colleague in the weekly meeting the way we always do, we can plan to ask a new question or respond in a different way. Then we can see how that feels, potentially checking in with a trusted colleague who is also in those weekly meetings, to see how she perceived the exchange. Then we take all this information into reflection.

Many people see great benefit in reflection through peer coaching. The idea of peer coaching is built on the premise that providing structure and context for people to reflect together will prove to be an important learning opportunity in its own right. The Arbuckle Leadership Fellows Program at Stanford, which teaches second-year MBA students how to effectively develop others by coaching and mentoring first-year MBA students, is peer led. I remember being surprised at how much of the leadership curriculum was structured around sending students off to talk with one another. I thought, *Are these grad students really paying a hundred thousand dollars a year to talk to their classmates?* But the reality is that this method is more effective than traditional models. And besides, in my classroom, they're paying that same tuition to sometimes sit quietly and not speak at all!

I use a structured peer-reflection process for each learning module in my class as well. For example, in the class on purpose, I give my students a "life in thirds" exercise in which they are asked to reflect on their lives by telling their story, spending a few minutes on each third of their life (childhood, the next third, and the most recent third). Their group members then share the values they heard reflected in the narrative. The results of this simple exercise can be profound. My students are often shocked by how readily their classmates understand who they are and what they value.

Thinkers50 has ranked Umair Haque,[7] director of Havas Media Lab and author of *Betterness: Economics for Humans and the New Capitalist Manifesto—Building a Disruptively Better Business*, as one of the world's most influential management thinkers. He argues that the twenty-first-century advantage is about doing the stuff that matters the most—spending time on the things that are truly meaningful. Like reflection. Breaking through the industrial age's rusty, cracked ceiling won't happen by just doing more of the same. "What got you here," as world-renowned business coach Marshall Goldsmith said in his bestselling book of the same name, "won't get you there." Evolving means investing not just in action, but in deep, sustained, prolonged reflection. That's not to say you'll instantly solve every big problem just by reflecting, but you might get a tiny bit closer, and it's those small steps that count.

What Doesn't Work

Learning from our failures is valuable but it isn't easy. Research from Barbara Fredrickson[8] suggests that the negative feelings that accompany mistakes and failures can interfere with the process of learning. When failures are emotionally painful they are less likely to be discussed, and learning from these experiences is harder to do.

In part, this may be due to the fact that our fight-or-flight response is triggered by frightening situations. This physiological response can make us want to literally run away from our failure or sometimes just ignore it. It can also prompt us to fight it—meaning rationalize it, blame someone else, or pretend it didn't happen. When we are continually triggered by stress or negative events, we can get stuck in this system, and it is bad for our mind, our nervous system, and our health.

Let's not forget that despite the popular embrace of the "fail better" mantra, failure in itself does not necessarily guarantee future success. Still, there are factors that make us more likely to learn from failure and move forward. For business school professors Yamakawa, Peng, and Deeds,[9] this became a research question. The three studied failed Japanese businesses and interviewed the entrepreneurs behind them to find out which mental factors led to positive outcomes post-failure. They found that the entrepreneurs' perceptions of the failures were a key determinant of their success in future endeavors. There was no direct correlation between the failed business and the success of a current business. The difference, the researchers found, was in the ability of the failing entrepreneur to accept responsibility and feel in control of the situation. These qualities prompted what is known as counterfactual thinking, or the considering of alternate possibilities. In other words, the process of pulling apart what went wrong needs to start with a fundamental willingness to accept responsibility, not just blame other people or chance. Then, with this in place, reflecting on the scenario and possible alternatives will position the entrepreneur to take on future opportunities successfully.

SELF-CRITICISM

In my class, I assign my students a design thinking–inspired exercise. Armed with whiteboard markers, they all go up to the front of the room at once and write out how they responded to a specific example of failure. Then they take a step back and read one another's stories, and begin building off them. For example, one student put an infinity symbol next to Netflix; another said he wanted to quit after getting a date wrong on a presentation. Their classmates draw bubbles and mark slashes to indicate "me too"—and from there, we have a discussion. What is interesting is that out of dozens of comments on the board, there are usually only two that are positive or even neutral about seeing failure as an opportunity to learn. We often see reactions such as "I wanted to quit" and notes about being ashamed, angry, or stressed. Most of the time, students are surprised (and relieved) to find that their high-performing classmates also felt inadequate and alone in their failures.

Learning to respond to and reflect more skillfully on our own failures involves unlearning habits of self-criticism that prevent us from opening our hearts and changing our behavior. A nonjudgmental attitude can be especially elusive at work, where results matter, performance is reviewed, and perfectionism is often secretly (or not so secretly) valorized. We all have a voice of self-criticism and self-hate ("I knew I would screw this up!" or "Now everyone thinks I'm an idiot"). I'm reminded of a story my husband once told me about a colleague. The man sat near him at their architecture firm in Boston and would repeatedly mutter, "Fuck, fuck, fuck," throughout the day as he was working. We laughed about it at the time, joking about how intense this guy was, but the reality is, he was probably just vocalizing what many people around him were thinking all day long.

RUMINATION

Students laugh out loud when I tell them the literal definition of *rumination*: "chewing the cud." I like this definition because, while it might sound more applicable to cows than humans, it cuts to the heart of the nature of rumination: mindless repetition.

The psychological trait of ruminating refers to repetitive thinking about negative topics (typically self-oriented) and is a key feature of depression and anxiety. More recently,[10] it has also been tied to health issues such as cardiovascular disorders.[11] Rumination (angry or sad) prolongs the heart's work in reaction to stress. It has been described as addictive. One of my students used the word *recycling* to illustrate what it feels like when she gets stuck in the negative feedback loop of a particular story or thought. Unlike reflection (a process in which you thoughtfully consider a given situation without judgment), rumination tends to focus only on what has gone wrong and why it is your fault. Rumination is reflection gone awry.

The neuroscience of rumination, drawn from the synthesis of a number of studies, was articulated in *Biological Psychiatry, 2015,* and the National Academy of Sciences by Stanford psychologist Paul Hamilton.[12] Hamilton suggests that when we become caught up in a cycle of rumination, the default neural patterns in our brains are disrupted.[13] Typically, when you're not focused on a task—when you're daydreaming or simply relaxing—your brain has a specific loop it automatically plays. In the case of rumination, it becomes increasingly connected to a region of the cerebrum known as the subgenual prefrontal cortex (sgPFC). In recent years, research has revealed that ruminative thinking follows a clear pattern. Scientists have observed increased blood flow in the sgPFC region of people who are depressed. Rumination keeps that region stuck in the activated mode, creating a default repeating circuit. This is the neural pattern of ruminators, whether depressed or not.

Hamilton's theory is that this increased connectivity between sgPFC and the default mode network in major depressive disorder is the effect of repeated self-referential thought patterns. Along with this neural cycle of a more highly activated sgPFC region, there emerges a pattern of behavioral withdrawal and negative emotional tone. This has been linked in research to repetitive thoughts of shame, anger, regret, and sorrow. Repetitive thinking makes us obsess about our mistakes instead of understanding them, learning from them, or fixing them. Studies have indicated that there is less operating memory in people who are depressed, and this may well be a result of the fact that their brains are hijacked by this cycle.

When I started meditating, I realized that in the early morning hours, when I was trying to sleep, I would get stuck in these ruminative cycles, basically chewing the cud of everything I had done wrong the day before, everything I didn't like about myself, and everything I would probably do wrong that day. I'd stay in restless sleep: falling asleep and then waking myself up with these thoughts again and again. It was exhausting and miserable.

When I started reflecting on these moments in my meditation practice, I realized that there was a baseline level of anxiety beneath the rumination. When I asked my teacher what I should do about it, I expected a profound answer. His response? Get up and run, then meditate—in that order. Move, get outside, physically break the loop. *Then* sit.

Reflecting means aerating our experience so we can break these loops. It helps us learn from failure and see the world beyond it instead of obsessing over it. This is meta-cognition. Mindfulness gives us the ability to track what the heck is going on with ourselves. It lets us see when we're recycling an idea and have moved from reflecting to repeating ourselves. When we realize we are doing this, we can break out of the pattern by placing our attention (and our bodies) elsewhere.

Self-compassion can help us soothe the underlying pain that got us stuck in the cycle of rumination. We narrate pain to ourselves again and again as an attempt to make ourselves feel better. Unfortunately, rumination doesn't make us feel better; it makes us feel worse. But self-compassion can get right at the underlying pain, and when we address that pain, we can then actually begin to heal.

PERFECTIONISM

How can we care deeply about our jobs, our families, our purpose, our effect on the world, without falling into the trap of perfectionism?

Perfectionistic striving is the belief that we should understand everything easily and be able to achieve our goals in just the right way and on the first try. There are two parts to perfectionism. The first is striving and setting extreme standards for our performance. The second part is the fear of negative evaluations or outcomes after making all that effort.

Unrealistic expectations stall us out from the incremental steps in thinking and action that enable us to grow and change. Perfectionism is the enemy of the practice of change making. When we have grand ideas for how we are supposed to be or act, ideas we can't or don't live up to, these concepts prevent us from taking reflective action in a better direction, one that is often gradual but nonetheless powerful in its impact.

In a 2016 meta-review of research on perfectionism[14] in a range of contexts, one takeaway was abundantly clear: perfectionism and burnout are closely related, particularly in the context of work. According to the authors of the study, perfectionism fuels stress, and burnout is the response to this chronic, high level of stress.

"Perfect" is the enemy of starting, evolving, and learning. I've found that getting people to recognize and overcome their perfectionistic tendencies through gentle reflection often leads to breakthroughs that help them connect with the reality of their lives and their own perfect imperfection. It helps them work with less pain. (It also helps them be a lot less painful to the people around them!) For example, sharing drafts of work with teammates or people whom we report to, rather than finished versions, can help us remove the burden of having to create something perfect. "Perfect" is daunting.

That said, reflecting and learning are part of a process—it isn't all "aha" moments and breakthroughs. If we expect catharsis in every instance of reflection in our learning endeavors, we are destined to be disappointed. Growing is uncomfortable. We have to stretch beyond our familiar ways of interpreting and acting. But if we can translate our caring about what we do from perfectionism and into problem-solving actions that we can take as individuals and communities, we will be much better equipped to make meaningful change that supports our purpose and values.

What Does Work?

I always tell my oldest child, "Don't just tell your little brothers what they did wrong. Tell them what they can do!" So, what *can* we do to reflect and learn from our failures, when we find ourselves spinning out over perceived or actual mistakes? We can invoke the common humanity mind-set.

It starts with paying attention. Notice when you are beating yourself up and try to shift your attention toward taking responsibility and fixing the situation. Reflection helps us clarify what works, what doesn't work, and which actions generate what effects (both our own actions and the actions of people around us) in a daily way. This is where prompts fit in. We design and redesign prompts for our pain points, to remind us to practice what we are intending to practice. And we create thought and behavior experiments that allow us to push beyond (even just a little) our usual habits and see what happens.

For example, you might ask another person for his input and perspective on a situation and share a little bit of what you're struggling with—a small dose. Does the world end? Are you exposed as a fraud or fired? If not, what does happen? Perhaps you'll learn a different way of dealing with a recurring problem or begin to look forward to the meeting you dread each week.

This is part of the art of remaining curious, being authentically interested in the world and the people around you, and being invested in your own growth. It is a deeply purposeful way of being that helps us be better workers, but it also goes way beyond productivity metrics.

POSITIVE SELF-TALK

I've already spent an entire chapter on self-compassion, but in the context of reflection and learning from experience, the key points are that we need to stop beating up on ourselves and start taking radical responsibility. The radical piece here includes the self-compassionate twist, not the jump-out-the-airplane-exit-door kind.

Notice the tone of voice you use with yourself when you realize you're mortified. Are you yelling at yourself? Calling yourself names? Are you getting on to solving the issue or staying stuck in repeating the script of railing against yourself?

It may seem at first glance that the language we use and the stories we tell ourselves about ourselves as we move through our day don't really matter. Actually, they make a huge difference! If we are abusing ourselves day in and day out, using hateful, biting language and an admonishing tone with ourselves, harsher than any we would use with another person, we are impacted by it. And when we are able to recognize this through mindfulness, it might lead to even more pain—at least until we realize that we can change it. And change it we can, through learning to apply a compassionate mind-set toward ourselves.

RADICAL RESPONSIBILITY

In order to have a growth mind-set, you need to take as much responsibility for yourself as you can. The first step is not to blame others when blame isn't clear. When things start to go south in the work-place, there is a tendency for people to scatter to their departments and hide behind their titles. Call it CYA (cover your ass) syndrome. Everyone is so afraid of being tainted by failure that they almost en-sure that a challenged project will fail. Instead, could compassion help us all see the problem as a common one? Instead of reacting with fin-gerprinting or "not me," how about if everyone held hands to fix the problem? Think of the idea of purpose: Is it your purpose at work to get this thing right or to *be* right? Which matters more?

If the company's sales are down, blaming the analytics team for its subpar reports, or the sales team for failing to reel in a big client, or the marketing team for not creating the right materials, doesn't help to solve the problem, and it undermines everyone. Instead, look for the things you can control (because there's always something you can con-trol) and focus on those! Placing agency outside ourselves creates an external locus of control that cripples our ability to have self-efficacy. Anytime we catch ourselves shifting blame to others, we should re-call the *lojong* slogan "Drive all blames into one." Blame is the prompt that brings awareness to our self-centered default for how we explain the world and attribute errors. When we create stories to support our "blame" narrative, we not only construct incomplete truths, we also undermine our ability to work well. Not to mention, if we throw oth-ers under the bus when the error is ours, it will eventually come back to bite us. And in the meantime, until it does, we'll have that niggling discomfort of not acting in accordance with our intention.

OWN YOUR MISTAKES

It takes a lot of courage to own our mistakes. When we realize we've made an error, most of us are so mortified that we would love to hide or, if we can't hide, at least hide the error. But in the long run, this

doesn't feel good, and it also doesn't earn us the respect of our colleagues or create the network of strong relationships we need to succeed over time.

How do we go about owning the mistakes we've made if we aren't
in a forgiving environment or if our boss isn't especially compassionate? Some ways would be to implement weekly check-ins, give honest
but compassionate feedback, hold annual conversations as learning
opportunities, encourage teams to meet for post-project hashes, or
discuss progress along the way at certain milestones.

CORRECTIVE FEEDBACK

Many of us struggle with offering corrective feedback to direct reports
or peers, but the reality is that most people actually want our feedback. In a study that polled nine hundred employees,[15] researchers
asked participants whether they would prefer praise/recognition or
corrective feedback at work. A significantly larger number of employees (57 percent) said they would prefer corrective feedback; 43 percent
responded that they'd prefer praise/recognition. When asked what was
most helpful in their careers, 72 percent of employees responded that
their performance would improve if their managers provided corrective feedback.

People believe that constructive criticism is essential to their career
development; they want it from their leaders. But their leaders often
don't feel comfortable offering it. From this we conclude that the ability to give corrective feedback constructively is one of the critical keys
to leadership, an essential skill to boost your team's performance, and
one that could set you apart.

But don't assume that all people are unaware of their weaknesses.
Jack Zenger and Joseph Folkman,[16] who run a consultancy company,
wrote an article for *Harvard Business Review* in which they "asked a
global sample of 3,875 people who'd received negative or redirecting

feedback if they were surprised or had not known already about the problem that was raised. We were taken aback to discover that fully 74 percent indicated that they *had* known and were *not* surprised."[17]

The ratio of positive to negative feedback matters at work just as it does in marriage. Researcher Emily Heaphy at the Rhode Island College of Business studied teams to find out what role feedback plays in performance, and her findings uncannily echoed well-known psychologist John Gottman's analysis[18] of wedded couples' likelihood of getting divorced or remaining married. The single biggest determinant for success is the ratio of positive to negative comments the partners make to one another. And the optimal ratio is amazingly similar: five positive comments for every negative one. (For those who ended up divorced, the ratio was 0.77 to 1—or something like three positive comments for every four negative ones.)

Research also suggests that the underlying issue for optimal feedback conditions is psychological safety. People need to feel safe enough to listen, to work on their weak areas, to be vulnerable in sharing their growth process and getting support when they are stuck. The whole point of feedback is to learn and get better. But the ability to take in feedback and reflect on it means that we need to feel safe enough to hear it. If we feel safe with the person who offers us feedback and if we trust that his interest is in helping us improve rather than harming us or pinning his mistakes on us, we are in a position to learn and grow.

Accomplish This:
Applying Reflection Practices

The following practices are all forms of reflection. Some may work better for you at some times than others, but all can be integrated into your daily life.

– **Investigative reflection.** If a challenging thought arises, you can look into the nature of thought itself. Just like a detective on a case, you can ask questions to learn what's really going on. Who is thinking the thought? Where is the thought happening? This form of reflection turns our attention to the mechanics of our senses, how they function, and how thoughts and perceptions are formed.

– **Journaling (on paper or not).** Keeping a journal is a great way to reflect, but traditional pen-and-paper "journaling" is not a prerequisite for reflection. We can mentally journal anytime, anywhere—on our commute home, while sipping our morning coffee, while cooking dinner or doing the dishes. But we have to be honest with ourselves about whether we are actually doing it. For some people, keeping a physical journal and making a habit or ritual out of writing things down can help with that accountability. For others, having a reflection partner, someone you check in with periodically and with whom you share your reflections, is a helpful practice.

– **Free, unadulterated writing.** Just write. Put onto paper whatever is in your mind to clear out space for new experiences and new learning. Once the thoughts are out of your head, you can even crumple up the paper and recycle it. The symbolism of tossing it is powerful, and provides a sense of release. It's like Marie Kondo-ing your brain—the life-changing magic of reflection!—reminding us that thoughts are just thoughts: insubstantial, passing.

– **Visualization/Revisiting.** Visualization can be used with a technique called imagery exposure, which I liken to watching reruns of our experiences. In this exercise, you pick a distressing experience that is taking up mental real estate, such as getting negative feedback from a superior or peer. Bring this incident to mind and visualize it in all its detail—the physical surroundings, the smells, the language the person used—and identify the feelings (anger, fear, exposure) and thoughts that automatically accompany the situation. You can continue this process in prolonged imagery exposure until the level of distress you feel about the incident is about half what it initially felt like. There is also a version of exposure therapy that involves spending time in the context that was so distressing and staying there until the distress level decreases. For example, revisit the site where the incident took place. Revisit the behavior. Taking on the things we fear most, be it speaking up in a meeting or writing a report, helps our brain process the difficult thoughts and feelings that keep popping back up in a ruminative loop. It also diminishes avoidance and suppression of negative feelings because the intensity of the pain is diminished—it's not so overwhelming that it can't be handled anymore.[*]

 - **The Honey Don't List.** Another form of exposure therapy involves writing a list of the things you would normally avoid. I call this the Honey Don't List, likening it to the list we get from our partner of chores we'd rather avoid. A client with social anxiety, for example, might put asking someone on a date at the top of her list and asking someone for directions near the bottom of her list. For each item on your list, rate the level of distress you associate with the action. Use a scale from 0 to 10, with the highest value reflecting the most discomfort. (Sending an e-mail might rate a 0, but speaking in public might rate a 10.) Try to have several items at each distress level, so there are no big jumps. The idea is to work your way through the list from lowest level of stress to highest. You would likely experiment with each item several times over a period of a few days until the distress you felt about being in that situation was about half what it was the first time you tried it. Then move to the next item on the list.[†]

 - **Gratitude practice.** The concept of practicing gratitude has become immensely popular in recent years for its magical-seeming impact on health and well-being. Practicing gratitude makes a lot of sense if we think of it as a daily reminder to reflect (not ruminate) and specifically to

---

[*] Examples of guided imagery: www.leahweissphd.com/guided-imagery.

[†] Example of a "Honey Don't" list: www.leahweissphd.com/honey-dont.

include the positive in our world, the kindness of neighbors, the effort that goes into supporting the materiality of our experience. Also celebrating our own wins: my friend and mentor Jadah Sellner encouraged me to begin a thirty-day challenge today to celebrate my wins and what is going well professionally for me each day. This is to counteract my tendency always to focus on what could be improved, what is not working. Not that that isn't a good thing to do, but it needs to be balanced, and there's a lot to say for a strengths-based approach rather than a pathological approach to work/life.

– **Guided inquiry.** There are various distinct forms of reflection within Tibetan Buddhism. For example, there are guided inquiries in the *Madyamaka* training for monastics. They are asked to reflect on specific concepts, such as impermanence, suffering, the preciousness of our lives, and the law of karma (or cause and effect). Then, in a purification practice, they work with regrettable past actions by recollecting them and vowing not to do them again. Perhaps one of the distinct features of Tibetan Buddhism is the clarity with which it articulates the purpose of these types of reflection and how to do them.

– **Time in nature.** Research shows[19] that time spent in nature reduces rumination. Given that more than 50 percent of people now live in urban areas, getting access to nature is a real issue. By 2050, this proportion will be 70 percent. Spending even a small amount of time outside supports reflection, especially when, for many of us, the majority of the workweek is spent indoors.

Incorporating opportunities for and ways of practicing reflection isn't an all-or-nothing proposition. Behavioral change researchers repeatedly find that small incremental changes, when done repeatedly and consistently, win the day. So, in the context of our lives, that means making simple goals that we can execute day to day.

Reflection is not a path of dramatic change and breakthroughs.

It's a practice with pauses, nudges, and adjustments in the direction of our purpose. It's a path of intentional, incremental changes that add up to make a difference in how we think about and approach our work. At the end of the day, after a meeting, an e-mail exchange (anything we went into with an intention), we should pause to consider how it went and to reset our intention. We can do this skillfully and compassionately without getting lost in judgmental rumination. By reflecting on our experiences, we can learn from them and be more aware of our responses. With practice, we can stop wasting time and energy on mind-sets that don't serve our purpose or benefit our work.

8

How Courage Makes Us
More Resilient

COURAGE IS BEING SCARED TO DEATH—BUT SADDLING UP ANYWAY.

—John Wayne

Right before one of the space shuttle launches, an engineer who worked for NASA realized she had miscalculated the weight of the cargo that had been loaded onto the shuttle, creating a potentially dangerous situation for the astronauts on board. The engineer knew that if she reported this problem it would delay the launch and cost NASA around a million dollars. She also feared that such a mistake might mean the end of her career. There was, she considered, the possibility that everything would go fine and her mistake would never be found out. Yet the risk was too great—she knew she had to inform one of her supervisors of her error.[1]

Sadly, we all know of another shuttle launch where the errors resulted in tragedy. In the case of *Challenger*, several NASA employees tried to halt the launch. Engineer Bob Ebeling and four of his colleagues alerted supervisors to potential issues, but higher-ranking authorities dismissed their concerns and went ahead with the launch as planned. Thirty years ago, in an anonymous NPR interview—he feared using his name at the time—Ebeling recalled a "contentious prelaunch meeting" and "hours of data review and arguments." The data showed that the rubber seals on *Challenger*'s booster rockets wouldn't seal properly in cold temperatures and that this would be "the coldest launch ever." On the day of the launch, the seals failed, and *Challenger* blew up just a minute after take-off. All seven people on board were killed.

Ebeling retired soon after the tragedy, and by his own admission, he has never really recovered from it. Thirty years later, he discussed with NPR the grief, guilt, and depression he's struggled with for years. "There was more than enough [NASA officials and managers from seal maker Thiokol] there to say, 'Hey, let's give it another day or two,'" Ebeling recalls. "But no one did."

Just as it took tremendous courage for the engineer in the first story to speak up about the miscalculation of cargo weight, it took tremendous courage for Ebling and his colleagues to speak up on the brink of such a highly publicized shuttle launch with so much at stake. But the very different endings to these stories offer evidence that, unless it is coupled with decisive action, courage amounts to little more than good intention. So how do we make our courage count?

Elements of Courage

Aristotle said, "Courage is the first of human virtues because it makes all others possible." Virtues are the ideals we strive to live by. But even when we have the best intentions, it can prove challenging to incorporate our values into our actions. Why is this the case?

University of Pennsylvania psychologist and founder of the Positive Psychology movement, Martin Seligman,[2] has revolutionized and quantified the study of courage. Together with Dr. Christopher Peterson, an expert in the field of hope and optimism, Seligman has studied across cultures and examined a wide variety of religious and philosophical texts to classify and measure what the two call the Values in Action Inventory of Strengths. Courage, considered valuable in almost every culture, is defined by Seligman as the "will to accomplish goals in the face of internal or external opposition."

Although courage has long been valued in wisdom traditions and philosophy, research on what courage really is, and how to cultivate it, is still emerging. But one point on which everyone seems to agree is that there are three crucial elements to courage: a morally worthy goal (according to "universally" held moral beliefs); intentional action; and perceived risks and obstacles that threaten both the implementation of action and the realization of the goal. So you have to identify a goal, take actions toward it, and endure the experience of the fear as part of that process.

By definition, then, without the experience of fear, there can be no courage. What is interesting about this is that we can develop our courage only when we are asked to stretch past our comfort zone. We can't grow more courageous if we shy away from the things that make us afraid. That means if we are afraid of speaking in groups, the only way through is to pipe up in meetings. If we are afraid to give direct feedback, we must practice doing just that.

Courage has two core components. The first is the courage inherent in facing external challenges and barriers for the purpose of acting with integrity. For example, Mona Hanna-Attisha,[3] a pediatrician in Flint, Michigan, was the first person to make the connection between the health problems experienced by her young patients and the high levels of lead in the city water. She tested the water herself and released her data at a press conference surrounded by her medical colleagues. She was harassed by community members, criticized by public officials, and scrutinized in the media. Though she suffered tremendous anxiety and illness as a result, Dr. Hanna-Attisha's first priority was the health and safety of her patients, so she continued her fight despite the dangers to herself. Thanks to her act of courage, the problem was addressed and actions are under way to remedy it as well as to hold accountable those complicit in the cover-up. Dr. Hanna-Attisha is now at the forefront of helping treat the more than eight thousand children who are suffering the consequences of lead poisoning.

The second component of courage is facing interior challenges. Acts of courage often force us to acknowledge our fallibility and take responsibility for continuing on a painful path of self-discovery. In this way even smaller actions, like engaging in contemplative practices such as meditation and reflection, require courage. When I tell people I've attended silent retreats that last for several weeks, I often get a response of shock or disbelief. They can't imagine how frightening or boring it would be to spend day after day, week after week, with only their own minds for company. (Though, to be honest, there is a community aspect to these group retreats. Having company to face ourselves and our fears is immensely helpful.) This makes me think of an Anne Lamott quote: "My mind is like a bad neighborhood, I try not to go there alone."

With practice, however, we can get better at tolerating the sensation of fear as well as the objects of our fear. When we become more intimate with fear, we can withstand its physiological expression. (That constriction in our chest means we are frightened, not dying.) If we are *too* afraid to feel fear, then we can't move to the next step of gaining a tolerance to the things that make us afraid. Humans can build up such an aversion to the object we fear that we will go to great lengths to avoid it. This avoidance of the fear then becomes its own kind of suffering. Facing the fear can mean just turning toward it rather than away from it, and maybe not even stepping toward it at all. It doesn't require diving in whole hog. It means stretching beyond your circle of comfort. If you are afraid of public speaking, you don't have to start by signing up to give a talk in front of five hundred people. You could start by setting an intention to speak up more often in your daily meetings. Once that feels comfortable, you could test your courage a little further, maybe giving a presentation to a small group of trusted colleagues—and build from there. So having courage means not only overcoming the thing we are afraid of, but also learning to engage with the fear itself.

The more we practice being courageous and acting in the face of fear, the better we get at it. And the more we don't act courageously and the more we stay entirely within the confines of our comfort zones, the harder it becomes to muster courage when it is needed. To build a courageous character, you must continually strengthen the muscle of courage. Aristotle said that we develop courage by performing courageous acts. Recent psychological research also suggests that courage is a habit we develop by repeated acts of bravery. This might take the form of having a difficult conversation with a boss or colleague, working toward an intimidating goal, changing jobs, or even doing something personally challenging, such as training for a race or learning how to ski.

Accomplish This: Taking Inventory of Fear

Taking Inventory of Fear

Sometimes we grow so accustomed to our fears (and avoiding them) that we don't realize how much they are holding us back. Take a moment to consider your fears at work and how they might be impacting you and those around you:

- Is there a difficult coworker whom you avoid?
- Is there a project you have wanted to pursue, but you have not yet been able to ask permission from your boss?
- Do you always glance away when people are looking for a leader or facilitator in a meeting, so as to not be called upon?

Now think about what simple steps you could take to face these fears:

- Could you invite the coworker to coffee?
- Might you draft a proposal for your boss, to get your thoughts on paper?
- Could you practice being a facilitator in a meeting that includes just a few of your trusted colleagues?

Clinical psychologist at Seattle Pacific University, Christopher Keller,[4] performed a study in 2016 examining the relationship between courage, psychological well-being, and physical well-being—and had some surprising findings. While previous research had linked courage with increased mental health, until Keller's study, little was known about the impact of courage on physical health.

Keller identified four different types of courage, including work/employment (dealing with workplace conflict or challenges, taking a career risk), religious/patriotic (taking a stand for one's ideals and beliefs), social/moral (taking action and putting oneself at risk socially, financially, or physically for a moral cause), and independent (acting altruistically toward others at a cost to oneself).[5]

Keller found that acting with courage predicts not only psychological well-being, but also physical well-being in the form of better neuroendocrine regulation—neuroendocrine is the overlap between the hormones and nervous system—improved immune functioning, reduced risk of cardiovascular disease, improved sleep, and improved cognitive function.[6] Acting courageously also was associated with less pain. In other words, having courage is a strong predictor of psychological and physical well-being. When we face the challenges of day-to-day life headfirst, we are healthier. When we lack courage—when we hide, don't act, or don't speak up—we are left to lead smaller, less purposeful lives and suffer the painful consequences of emotional suppression.

The good news is that studies show that many of us are courageous at work, especially when it comes to external challenges, such as witnessing sexual harassment or bullying. However, while 30 percent of employees observe illegal workplace actions and 80 percent have experienced or witnessed abusive behavior from bosses or coworkers, a very small percentage actually speaks up.

What makes one employee more likely or able to act with courage than the person in the next cubicle? Some researchers point to an individual's character. Others emphasize the role of the environment, context, and the culture in which the individual works. Psychologist Phil Zimbardo,[7] who conducted the famous Stanford Prison Experiment, says that, in his own research, he hasn't yet been able to pinpoint the factors that make someone a hero. Theories under consideration range from the existence of a "hero gene" to having higher levels of compassion. "Compassion is a virtue that may lead to heroism, but we don't know that it does," says Zimbardo. Another key insight from his research, he says, is that "heroes are most effective not alone but in a network. It's through forming a network that people have the resources to bring their heroic impulses to life."

An example of courage amplified, or perhaps enabled, by teamwork is Cynthia Copper, the former vice president of internal audit for the telecom giant WorldCom. Working at night with a team of colleagues, Copper investigated and exposed one of the worst examples of corporate fraud in history, to the tune of $3.8 billion. In 2002, *Time* magazine named her Person of the Year for her courage in speaking up, but her bravery didn't end there. Copper stayed with WorldCom for two more years, despite being an unpopular presence at work.

Healthy work environments allow employees to speak out against accepted ideas or norms. Some research shows that environments such as these are correlated with higher-producing teams. Teams that can speak up more earn more—to a point. There is an ideal level of calling each other out and holding each other accountable. Too much of this kind of feedback, though, is crazy-making and creates inefficiencies. It becomes impossible to get anything done in an environment that is *too* "open" or critique-driven. But a moderate amount of challenging is good for everyone and fosters acts of courage.

The truth is courage matters not only to employees, but also to the bottom line. One study[8] found that when employees don't feel comfortable speaking up, they're less satisfied at work. Absenteeism also increased, as did nonproductive work behaviors, low team identification, and eventually reduced performance and increased turnover. In another study, conducted at Cornell University,[9] only 51 percent of Fortune 100 employees said they felt safe speaking up at work, and as a result, the companies for which they work lose a combined $31.5 billion per year. The leadership training firm VitalSmarts found that it costs an employer $7,500 each time an employee doesn't speak up.[10] In their analysis, they summarized, "This study confirms what we've seen over the past 30 years: One of the costliest barriers to organizational performance is unresolved crucial conversations." If evidence like this isn't motivation enough to create safe work environments, I don't know what is.

Work environments that support psychological safety foster more productive teams and organizations. Research published in the *Journal of Applied Psychology*[11] shows that even when those who speak up and challenge the status quo aren't correct, "they cause the rest of the group to think better, to create more solutions, and to improve the creativity of problem-solving." The safety of the group is another key component of work environments that are conducive to acts of courage. When we feel supported by one another, we can retreat to the safety of the team if our ideas are challenged. "If group members trust each other, they will be more likely to accept stated disagreements at face value and less likely to misinterpret task conflict behaviors by inferring hidden agendas or personal attacks as the driving force behind the behavior . . . [On the other hand,] when group members do not trust each other, they are likely to interpret the ambiguous behavior of others negatively and infer relationship conflict as a plausible explanation for the behavior." Even if our work environment isn't organized around a team structure, having the support of our colleagues can allow us to act with courage when it is needed.

In 2014, following the scandals of WorldCom, Enron, and several other high-profile companies, three business school professors interviewed ninety-four business executives and military officers, mostly male, who worked for organizations such as NASA, the NFL, all four divisions of the armed forces, GE, and a few start-ups and hospitals, with the objective of identifying what makes some people stand up to authority. They found that "confronting one's superior directly appears to be, in participants' eyes, exceptionally risky." In their data, they found that "reported negative outcomes for the courageous actors came largely from events classified as standing up to authority (60 percent of standing up to authority incidents were reported as resulting in harm to the actor compared with just 26 percent of other incidents)."

There are good reasons to be afraid to speak up when we are in a culture that doesn't encourage or support ideas that go against the grain. Assistant professor of management at the University of Texas, Austin, Ethan Burris[12] researches the risks and rewards of speaking up. He conducted three experiments and one field study to examine how people view dissenting opinions from employees. He found that "employees who speak up and challenge the status quo are viewed as less competent, less dedicated to the organization, and more threatening compared to those who support the way things are."

Harvard Business School professor Amy Edmondson and Penn State professor James Detert[13] explored the challenges employees face speaking up to internal authorities and what organizations can do to foster these acts of courage. Their research focused on behavior in large multinational corporations, but the lessons learned can apply to smaller enterprises as well.

They identified two factors that lead people to feel more or less safe speaking up: individual differences and contextual factors. Individual differences include an individual's communications skills, level of extroversion or introversion, and other personality factors. Context is the external environment of an organization that either encourages or discourages input.

Don Juan, as quoted by Jack Kornfield in *A Path with Heart*, once said, "Only as a [spiritual] warrior can one withstand the path of knowledge. A warrior cannot complain or regret anything. His life is an endless challenge, and challenges cannot possibly be good or bad. Challenges are simply challenges. The basic difference between an ordinary man and a warrior is that a warrior takes everything as a challenge, while an ordinary man takes everything as a blessing or a curse."

Reflection helps us access our inner warrior. It allows us to see the gap between our intentions and our actions. It takes courage to be willing to look at the gap. As one of my students once put it, it takes courage to engage "the tension between a naturally open heart and the naturally wary mind." It is an act of bravery to pause, look at what we're doing and how we're suffering, and be honest about what we see. By that I mean acknowledging the things we don't like, the feelings that make us really uncomfortable, and the fears we have about who we are, what we're capable of, and how we are perceived.

Courage also prevents our becoming totally demoralized by what we see, so we don't abort our mission and return to the safety of habits that may be comfortable but that don't help get us where we really want to be. With courage, we can do something about our behavior and our attitudes, we can do things differently, we can try again.

As soon as we start a new course of action, we are going to encounter challenges—whether it is summoning compassion for an especially annoying coworker or dealing with the paperwork and legal mess of starting our own business. Purpose, when we put it into practice with mindfulness and compassion, makes us brave. As Julie Aigner-Clark, who founded the Baby Einstein Company, told *Forbes* in a 2014 interview,[14] "Fear and doubt are always the biggest obstacles in starting a business. Is my idea good enough? Will others want it? But I really believed in what I was doing."

The more we can anticipate setbacks, the readier we'll be to overcome them. But even if we anticipate challenges, the fact is that sometimes we'll fall into old habits. We'll snap at that annoying coworker whose support we need on a big project, or we'll avoid doing the paperwork that makes our head hurt.

Even everyday goals can pose challenges. I have a lime-green sticky note above my desk that reads, "Stay focused and off e-mail!" But some days I just don't follow that advice. I also have a plan A for enjoying a long morning routine, and a backup, shorter plan B in case plan A is thwarted. Still, instead of our intentional start to the day, we'll dive into e-mail, and the next thing we know, we've run out of time to work on what really matters. This is not the image we want of ourselves. But we do have a choice: to try to understand what led us to spend our time in a way we didn't feel good about, to take responsibility for our state of mind and our actions—or to do nothing. This is hard. This is uncomfortable. This requires courage.

To get from here to there, we must reflect on what's driving our behavior. This requires an amount of accountability that is not easy to summon. It means not blaming other people or the situation for what went wrong, but instead pointing the finger at ourselves—to "drive all blames into one," as the *lojong* slogan goes.

Accomplish This: Staying on Track

Articulating our goals and then ensuring we spend time making progress toward them is important to achieving our purpose. It takes courage to take accountability of our shortcomings and to change actions that lead to more fulfilling outcomes.

Try practicing the following exercise to stay on track:

- What's written on the proverbial sticky note on your desktop? What are the goals or aspirations that help you connect to your larger purpose or that just curb anxiety-inducing behaviors? If you don't actually have a sticky note in your work space, consider creating one and putting it within easy eyeshot.
- Spend time observing the ways you typically fall short of your goals on a daily or weekly basis.
- Now take time to reflect on the gap between what you want to do and what takes you off track.
- The next time you have an urge to engage in behavior that takes you away from your goals, such as spending an hour on e-mail rather than working on a proposal you are excited about, practice redirecting your attention.

What does it take to have courage in this way? Remember our three elements of courage: a morally worthy goal, intentional action, and perceived risks, threats, and obstacles. It takes knowing that we are afraid and not defaulting to avoidance behaviors. It takes recognizing that our thoughts are just thoughts and that a fearful thought need not be heeded. Being courageous means being aware that we are afraid but facing our fear and acting toward our goal anyway. As I tell my six-year-old when she's afraid, being courageous doesn't mean we aren't afraid. It means that we don't let our fear stop us. But we have to disbelieve our thoughts. And we need to have something else to rely on, such as our purpose, that will see us through the action.

Our purpose connects the days, hours, and moments of our work to something greater than the sum of its parts. When we are bolstered by the sense that we are part of something meaningful, we are more willing to take risks, have difficult conversations, and accept responsibility rather than place blame. We are more likely to do the hard thing when we remember why it matters that we do it at all.

Courage Takes Practice

One of the lessons from psychology research is that repeated exposure to scary situations builds courage. Both practicing something (or the steps that lead to that something) in real life or rehearsing it mentally can prepare us to act courageously when we are afraid. It may seem like a herculean task, but the practice is essential.

There are a million different ways we can train to be more courageous. And courage means a lot of different things. It is not only the courage to run into the burning building. It can also be the courage to try to take the perspective of someone who has an experience different from our own. Courage could mean dropping protecting ourselves— from criticism, from staying in our safe zone. There are many ways to become more courageous: face your demons, be more vulnerable, be honest, give feedback, and persevere, which requires ongoing effort. Courage is something we need to practice all the time as part of living purposeful lives.

Managerial Moral Courage

Moral courage is the ability to act rightly in the face of popular opposition, discouragement, hardship; to stand up for the principles
you believe in and care about. At the University of Quebec,[15] Michelle
Harbour and Veronika Kisfalvi have studied what they call "managerial moral courage." They've classified two types of managerial courage: the courage to act and the courage to be. Their findings reveal
that managers consider courage to have a moral dimension. In other
words, they see decision making as having an ethical response to risky
or difficult situations. In addition to self-confidence and a strong ego,
managers need to seek out "support, regulation strategies, and trans-
fer of responsibility . . . in order to sustain their managerial moral
courage in difficult and intensely emotional moments." Their research
also shows that courage is a highly regarded virtue and considered
crucial for today's leaders and managers.

One way for us to become more courageous is to look at courage
as a skill that can be developed. Kathleen K. Reardon, a professor of
management and organization at the University of Southern California's Marshall School of Business, wrote a piece for the *Harvard
Business Review* on how courage is tied in with decision-making skills
and how you can develop it. She makes the distinction between pro-
fessions such as police officer and firefighter (both of whom risk their
lives at work) and employees in business settings. After interviewing
more than two hundred senior and midlevel executives, she found that
managerial courage involves calculated risk taking and decision making that improve over time with practice.

Reardon created the concept of a "courage calculation," identifying a six-step method that included setting goals and deciding
whether they are obtainable, setting secondary goals if the first goals

don't work, and determining the importance of the goal—meaning is it high priority? If it is of low priority, it may not be worth the risk, or, as she says, "Does the situation call for immediate, high-profile action or something more nuanced and less risky? Courage is not about squandering political capital on low-priority issues." Reardon also discusses tipping the balance of power in your favor by creating strong networks, weighing the risks against the benefits, selecting the proper time for action rather than rushing into a decision, and developing contingency plans so that you can be resourceful and persistent if things don't go as originally planned.

If you look only at her courage calculation, you can see the importance of mindfulness (as opposed to rash or hurried action) in decision making. When faced with a decision to do something or not, start by asking yourself, "Is it possible?" Then ask, "Is it important?" Then: "Can I go about it in a low-key way or does it necessitate a public confrontation?" While you ask yourself these questions, notice how you are feeling. Are you unregulated? Where in your body are you feeling this? Using mindfulness can help you to acknowledge your mental, emotional, and physical state. It doesn't mean you won't sometimes act while you're freaked out, but more often than not, having clarity on how you are feeling can stop you from making a rash decision, such as quitting your job over something that wasn't actually a high-purpose issue to you.

It's important to remember that courage isn't just an individual quality; it is something reinforced or undermined by our social context and professional environment—there is a powerful social element to the workplace. When people witness courage, talk about it, or hear about it, they feel empowered to be courageous themselves. When they work in a culture of fear, they are reluctant to act with courage.

Some research on organizational courage has determined that the phenomenon of "emotion contagion" (the notion that emotion travels through groups; that if one person feels an emotion, the rest of the group will experience that same emotion) also plays a role in workplace cultures. "Once courage is successfully encouraged and instilled among a few individuals," Ralph Kilmann of the University of Pittsburgh says, "the social dynamics of organizations mean that the practice can more easily become an organizational virtue." This occurs because "courage is socially contagious: courage has impact through the feelings of moral elevation in the members who witness the acts, and through social exchanges and organizational stories."

One way to foster courage in the workplace is to model it at the executive level. Leaders who are courageous enough to be honest and transparent inspire workers to do the same. This is true of our most iconic and beloved leaders—the Martin Luther Kings and Aung San Suu Kyis of the world—but examples can also be found in everyday workplaces. It is also true for the Dropbox leadership, who came back from a retreat in which they'd shared their own weaknesses and asked to be called out when they backslid, in the name of growing themselves, in growing trust in the teams, in cultivating this willingness in others.

Part of being transparent as a leader is being open to receiving feedback. It is way too tempting to hide from ourselves. The willingness to tell others our mistakes (to confess, as it were) is the start of the process of taking responsibility and making change. To open ourselves to hearing how we are being perceived by others, even when it is scary or unpleasant, requires a great amount of courage. We see this outside of the workplace in the form of recovery/twelve-step programs; *sangha*, or spiritual/personal growth communities; group therapy; and Lean In Circles—all these are examples of the power of accountability and feedback. In order for organizations to flourish, they must create systemic support systems for employees.

Accomplish This: Motivating with Purpose

How do you motivate those around you? Do your talks about the bottom line, about quarterly metrics, or team goals also address the fundamental motivations of the people with whom you are working? Are there specific aspects of your company's mission or service that you can focus on? Or can you take the opportunity to better understand the meaning the work has for your teammates by learning:

- Why they are excited about a particular project;
- What skills or knowledge they might gain as a result of the work;
- How the work allows people to create better lives for themselves or their families

The more you understand what motivates team members, the better you can tap into their ability to connect with their purpose and drive meaningful results.

100 Percent Responsibility

Diana Chapman, a dynamic executive coach and the coauthor of *The Fifteen Commitments of Conscious Leadership*, teaches what she calls "100 percent responsibility," which is one of her commitments of conscious leaders. She has made the idea popular in the YPO world and beyond.

In YPO, or the Young Presidents' Organization, when someone is late to a meeting, he may well end up getting called out in front of the group, to take ownership for the choices he made that caused him to be late. The idea is that even if there was crazy traffic, he could have made different choices that would have allowed him to arrive on time. The logic is that lateness is not something that *happens to you* but, rather, a setup you create with your own choices.

Such challenges allow people to take responsibility for their role in a problem and to acknowledge their agency and ability as having an impact on the situation. Think of responsibility as a pie: owning our share ("driving all blames into one") can be a corrective for the feeling many of us have that we are at the mercy of forces at work and in our private lives, particularly the "forces" of other people's perceived wrongness and ineptitude. As Chapman says, practicing 100 percent responsibility does not mean being a control freak, or being naïve about the limits of our control. It means that we always have choices, that there is always something we can do that will impact our situation, starting with the way we view that situation. In the responsibility experiment, we practice with "opposite stories," taking blame that we could (or have) put on someone else, for example, and turning it into its opposite: a story about what we could have done or, more important, can do. We always have the power to affect (which is not to say control) our destinies. We can't all be CEOs—most of us wouldn't want to!—but we can be influencers. We are all leaders in some context—at work, at home, or ultimately as leaders of our own lives.

Taking responsibility requires courage. Being accountable, refraining from blaming others, and focusing on what is within our control—it is a lot more challenging than we might initially suspect. The social model of interaction known as the drama, or Karpman, triangle (which I use in my class and is used in YPO, among other places) focuses on our habit of moving from victim to hero and casting others in complementary roles. It was originally developed by Stephen Karpman, MD, as a tool for illustrating the connection between responsibility and power, and their relationship to boundaries. When people interact, they can fall into the role of the Persecutor (or Villain), the Rescuer (or Hero), or the Victim. The idea is to take responsibility for your own role and to turn it from a passive and into an empowered position for the greater good of the group.

We need to own our locus of control. We need to take responsibility for our minds, our attitudes, our relationships, our actions. According to the research on self-efficacy and internal/external locus of control, we can be courageous (i.e., switch to owning our influence in our lives), we can lead our own lives, whether we are the CEO or at the lowest rung on the organization ladder. We may not be able to control the external by decree if we don't have overt power, but we can control the internal, and we can influence others. Still, this requires baseline courage and a willingness to assess our own role and the options we have within our control, and to focus on those rather than on placing blame. We have agency over our mind-set whether we are someone rising through the ranks, or a janitor at the hospital who chooses to recognize that she is an integral part of the care team.

By relating to coworkers with compassion, as fellow human beings and teammates rather than threats, we can tackle work with the strength of many people instead of one—and find that we have more resources to fight the good fight because we're not wasting those resources on the bad. Instead of the distraction of watching our backs, we are encouraged by people having our backs.

I like and use Karpman's model because it is an interesting practice in the context of recognizing our own stories and whether we are allocating agency to ourselves or externally. Also, it can help us see our pattern of blaming others.

The danger with this perspective, though, is it could be used to blame other people. Clearly, not everyone has the same flexibility in their time or roles that would allow them to move about the world exactly as they would choose. So, if we take this up, it should be a looking-in-the-mirror practice, not a way to blame others. The danger with the YPO set is that they do have the privilege of running their work lives in a way that most people don't. So it is important that assigning 100 percent responsibility doesn't turn into sneaky blaming.

In the context of the *lojong* slogan "drive all blames to one," the "one" refers to ego clinging. The one to be blamed (not other people/conditions) is our own narrow focus on ourselves, which is caused by our mistakenly identifying with a dualistic sense of self. In English, this means that we are so restricted in our viewpoint most of the time that we tend to blame others when things go wrong. To change that pattern, we practice driving all blames into our own ego clinging. This doesn't mean beating up on yourself. It means taking responsibility, seeing that the pattern of getting defensive and covering our asses is not the only way to move through the world. Each time we catch ourselves blaming, we can practice taking responsibility.

For your own practice, every time you find yourself about to blame another person, for anything, catch yourself and flip the blame around, experimenting with mentally taking responsibility. What does that feel like? Try to approach this exercise with curiosity, not judgment.

Ask yourself:

Am I taking full responsibility for my physical, emotional, mental, and spiritual well-being and renewal?

Am I supporting others in taking full responsibility for their well-being and renewal?

Or:

Am I blaming others or myself for what is wrong in the world?

Am I choosing to play the victim, rescuer, or persecutor, taking more or less than 100 percent responsibility for my life?

Once we have more clarity about our role in any given situation, we can make an intentional choice about the best next steps. It all starts with the courage to challenge our assumptions and open ourselves to vulnerability.

Accomplish This:
Cultivating Responsibility

Performance-focused training company VitalSmarts has conducted extensive research on the ways in which courage and accountability impact performance. Based on this data, they've come up with key recommendations employers can offer their employees to encourage them to act with courage:

1. **Change your thinking.** Instead of thinking about the risks that come from speaking up, think about the risks that come from not voicing your concerns.

2. **Defuse your emotions.** Many important conversations fail because the emotions that arise obscure the words being communicated. Try to enter a dialogue with the assumption that the other person is a rational, reasonable human being. Not only will this help you to focus on their words, it will also help you to come across as collaborative and agreeable.

3. **Make others feel secure.** When sensitive topics are discussed, many people become defensive. To get those in your interaction to feel safe, start critical conversations by assuring others of your positive intentions and your respect for them. When people feel respected and trust your motives, they are more likely to let their guards down and listen.

4. **Encourage discussions.** Once you have created a safe environment, make sure the other person understands that it is okay to disagree with you. Those who are best at holding crucial conversations don't just try to push their opinions on others; they also learn from those with whom they are speaking.

9

Purposeful Organizations

WHEN YOU'RE SURROUNDED BY PEOPLE WHO SHARE A PASSIONATE
COMMITMENT AROUND A COMMON PURPOSE, ANYTHING IS POSSIBLE.

—Howard Schultz, CEO of Starbucks

It's one thing to practice purposefulness at the individual level. As employees (and as people), we have the freedom to choose how we respond to challenges in the workplace. We can choose to be more compassionate, to cultivate courage, to heed the wisdom of our emotions. And we know that the social context of the workplace allows for our attitudes and actions to go viral—when we choose to act mindfully, we are bound to influence the people around us to act in kind.

For example, Chade-Meng Tan was one of the original engineers at Google and currently holds the role of Jolly Good Fellow, a title meant to spark a smile but one that allows him the opportunity to serve as the spokesperson for a mindful culture within and beyond the company. After studying and implementing mindfulness on a personal level, Tan brought the tenets of mindfulness to the company's attention. The management liked what they heard, and the result was a mindfulness-based stress reduction course designed for engineers.

The optional course began on a small scale in 2007, but Tan was able to recruit enough people from Google to expand it, and now a few hundred attendees are enrolled annually. Over the years Tan has been offering it, he's worked with thousands of people—a small percentage of Google's total size, perhaps, but notable nonetheless. It's a good example not only of the impact and effectiveness of peer-led coaching, but also of how the passion and purpose of one employee can infiltrate and influence an entire corporate culture. Tan's story serves as a grassroots guide of how to get it done without the resources of a CEO-level position.

This is one way to begin to heal the toxic workplace—from the bottom up, so to speak. But in addition to peer-led efforts, leader-initiated approaches can also be highly effective. And both of these strategies can be supported by programmatic efforts and can lead to real, measurable cultural changes.

The question is: what does mindfulness look like at the organizational level? How can businesses be more systemically mindful?

I recently sat down with the dean of Stanford Business School, Jonathan Levin, to talk about this very subject. To ask him: How do we recognize an organization that has gotten the soft skills right and what are the criteria by which we can even begin to base our assessment? In other words, how do we know what constitutes a purposeful organization?

I mentioned a few core capacities I teach, such as self-awareness, focus, prioritization, transparency, and compassionate candor. I then asked Dean Levin to share examples of companies that he believes exemplify these qualities.

He told me about some organizations that have developed unique cultures in which the leadership actively seeks to embed qualities like mindfulness into their processes. One of these organizations is Bridgewater, the largest hedge fund in the world, which manages $150 billion in global investments.

Leader-Initiated Approaches

Bridgewater has been on my radar for some time. I've actually assigned my students to watch videos of the organization's CEO, Ray
Dalio, discussing the role of meditation in his own personal success as
well as his organization's operating principles.

In the video, Dalio says that he starts his day at the office by turning
his chair away from the glass window to his office and meditating for
twenty minutes. His employees are encouraged to do the same. He has
also helped to create a culture in which the core principles of radical
transparency and candor are encouraged on a personal, interpersonal,
and organizational level.

Thus, employees are encouraged not only to be candid but also to
demand candor from one another. Radical transparency, as described
by Dalio, is "healthy loyalty [that] fosters improvement through openly
addressing mistakes and weaknesses." He explains why this benefits
his organization: "The more people are open about their challenges,
the more helpful others can be. In an environment in which mistakes
and weaknesses are dealt with frankly, those who face their challenges
have the most admirable character. By contrast, when mistakes and
weaknesses are hidden, unhealthy character is legitimized." In other
words, the best decisions cannot be made when people are withhold-
ing information because they are intimidated to speak out when it is
uncomfortable.

In his recent TED talk, Dalio endorsed the concept of radical transparency as a key quality of an effective organization. An organization
can only make good decisions when it has access to as many view-
points as possible. It's an appealing idea but it's not an easy one to put
into practice. As Dalio describes it, doing so can be "emotionally difficult" and takes practice. He emphasizes that the best way to go about
improving this capacity is to "observe yourself in conversations with

others," grow your self-awareness, pay attention to your communication habits, consider the benefits of expressing yourself more candidly, and keep in mind while these new behaviors might feel awkward at first, the upside for you and for the organization more than offsets this challenge.

Another example Dean Levin cited was Christopher Forman, the CEO of the real estate company Decurion Corporation. He views Forman as a leader who is striving to create a conscious business culture. A GSB alumnus, Forman has a distinctive leadership style. For example, when his employees need to resolve an issue, the company protocol is for everyone involved in the situation to sit in the middle of a circle and deal with the problem directly.

Of course, the sitting-in-a-circle approach isn't necessarily for everyone, but Forman has made it work, which has resulted in leadership development, emotional development, and productive interpersonal dynamics throughout the company. By employing a set of processes that makes direct communication a respectful and productive process, Forman has engendered a professional culture that attracts employees who appreciate this type of transparency and collaborative approach to problem solving.

It should also be noted that Bridgewater and Decurion are conventionally successful companies, at the top of their respective industries, which would suggest that their core values of being flexible, creative, and resilient in the face of challenges are beneficial (or at least not mutually exclusive) with organizational success. By encouraging their employees to focus on their own shortcomings and to be vulnerable and open in addressing them, workers grow as people and organizations flourish.

Undoubtedly, there is a movement underfoot in top MBA programs to include classes that train soft skills—alongside my class there are examples of courses targeting emotional intelligence and mindfulness at Harvard, Yale, Columbia, and many other universities. There is also a movement within top companies to include soft skills training as part of executive and staff development.

Success in integrating these high impact soft skills will mean different things for different organizations. Not everyone wants to record their failures or mistakes in an issues log for all to see, or have employees share their negative feelings with a "pain button" via an iPad app—and that's okay. Depending on the industry, the culture, and the goals of the organization, metrics will be designed differently. A health care company, for example, might measure the impact of mindfulness and compassion by tracking rates of increasing patient satisfaction and reducing medical error, whereas a hedge fund is likely to be focused on decision making and dollars earned.

When a company's leadership determines that a specific skill set or competency is important to its mission or culture, one way they go about educating employees is via mandatory training. As far as I am aware, there aren't currently any mandatory programs that incorporate mindfulness-based training. Given the data that supports mindfulness as an asset to both employee retention and happiness as well as a company's bottom line, I have to wonder if this isn't an untapped opportunity.

Another way to integrate mindfulness from a top-down approach is to use mindfulness-based principles in the recruitment process.[*] For example, tech giant LinkedIn holds compassion as a core company value and hires against it. They ask potential new hires how they would respond to tough choices between human well-being and the financial bottom line.

Using hiring practices that prioritize qualities like compassion

---

[*] Here, unlike in chapter 3, the terms *top-down* and *bottom-up* are being used in the context of management versus employees, in which "top-down actions" refer to those actions made by management and "bottom-up actions" to those made by employees.

gets more people in the door who are likely to be a fit with a culture that explicitly walks the walk on key values. But once they're hired, how can employers keep those values alive? The best leaders give their workers opportunities—and choices. For example, Mark Benioff, the CEO of Salesforce, lives and breathes mindfulness, and he wanted to incorporate it as a core value of his company. The Salesforce offices feature meditation rooms that are open to all, but not mandatory to any. He also brings in speakers like Thich Nhat Hahn, but attendance at these talks is optional. Practices like this are not only respectful of individual choices and values, but are also more likely than "required" activities to have the intended impact.

When I was brought into Google to consult on how to better incorporate mindfulness practices into their workplace, we looked at how we might influence the rituals and systems already in place—from the lunchroom setup to human resources policies. We asked ourselves: How can we create an initial spark of interest in compassion practice and then fan that spark into a much larger flame? We wanted to make sure our outreach felt relevant to the majority of employees who are unlikely to sign up for a meditation course—or those who might take it but ultimately don't find meditation to be a fit for their lifestyle.

The health care company Aetna is another organization that integrates corporate values from the top down. CEO Mark Bertolini created the role of CMO, or Chief Mindfulness Officer, and appointed a trusted colleague to run the company's mindfulness program. Creating this somewhat unorthodox role not only gives workers someone to reach out to if they are interested in learning about mindfulness-based skills and practices, it also sends a strong message about the organization's values.

Yet, even when the message is coming from the top, there are obstacles. Some employees might not feel entirely comfortable with the values being articulated from above. Organizations may also struggle to find the balance between mandatory and optional spaces/practices/

rituals. And of course, there is the biggest challenge: that mindfulness can't ultimately be whittled down to a course (mandatory or otherwise). In order to be effective, it must be woven into the fabric of the workplace. Meditating or meeting once a month won't do the trick— these practices have to be implemented consistently, on a daily basis, especially when things are busy and stressful.

Leader-Initiated Strategies for Integrating Mindfulness in the Workplace:

- Recognize the need for mindfulness in every facet of a company
- Assess opportunities in shared work spaces
- Address meeting practice flaws, and fix them
- Work toward creating a safe and secure environment for all employees
- Make mindfulness training just as important as HR training
- Incorporate mindfulness principles into company culture policies and documents
- Hire against criteria like compassion and service
- Find team weaknesses and address the gaps

The bad news is that our individual life experiences, responsibilities, and personal preferences will always make having a job a challenge sometimes. Our values and ethics, our background and feelings can't be checked at the door. There is no magical threshold that separates "work" and "life." All of it is a part of the same path. All of it fits somewhere into the picture of our puzzle box top.

The good news is that while our humanity may cause us pain at work, it also enables us to be better at our jobs and even allows the opportunity for us to thrive there. Because our histories, values, and goals—the very sources of our conflict and pain—are also an incredible resource for compassion, collaboration, and insight. But in order for these qualities to have a productive, positive influence on the work we do and the organizations for which we work, we have to move beyond tolerating or politely ignoring difference.

How we work and how we live matters. As individuals and as organizations, we must stand for human values, keeping in mind that we are human beings with human lives and bodies, even while we are at work and working. As workers we must take responsibility for our own sanity. We can't wait for our boss or HR director to do it for us. We have a great deal more influence over our situations than we often realize. And with this influence comes responsibility. We are accountable.

We all get to hold each other accountable whether we are executives or mid-level managers or entry-level employees. We all get to decide how well we allow one another to be treated in the world. And work counts as the world. You can demand respect of your coworkers, of your leaders, of yourself. You can stand up for integrity and compassion, even with the small stuff. And the way to do that is by facilitating and engaging in a purposeful culture.

When we do this, not only will our companies do better, but we will be better. We will perform better. The version of us that shows up at home in the evening will be a version our family and friends want to see. We will view our workdays as part of our big picture purpose, the one with a capital P.

We won't settle for lesser versions of ourselves or our work. We won't be perfect, but we'll be works in progress, working with intention, working toward meaning, and ultimately living meaningful lives.[1]

Acknowledgments

Enormous gratitude to the village it took to raise this book from idea to reality.

In particular, to my father, Andrew B. Weiss, MD, who taught me that how we work, especially with others, matters. I miss you every day. You never left my heart or mind. You never will. To David, my husband of almost ten years, who knows the wisdom of a good laugh. To my children and primary teachers, Beatrice, Caleb, and Isaac. The three of you have forever changed how I think about life, practice, work—and pretty much everything else.

To the rest of my amazing family, including my mom, Madge Weiss, who always said that education is *the* primary thing; and to my brother, Adam Weiss; and sister, Jennifer Weiss—two excellent examples of taking work as a path. Both of you have been crucial conversation partners along the way. To Lydia Callaghan (how do you always ask *the perfect* question?) and Jay Blecker (why am I never there when you do your famous dances?) and all my nieces and nephews—Madaleine, Faye, Lila, Colette, and Ryan—words can't express the gratitude I feel for having a family like you.

Pat Christen, thank you for being the kind of mentor and friend everyone should have in their corner. This book literally would not exist without you.

Thank you, Harper Wave (especially Julie Will) and my literary agent, Stephanie Tade, who took this glimmering idea and helped turn it into a reality. Enormous gratitude to Harriette Halepis and Ashley Abele, who are the dream team.

To Kelly McGonigal, Thupten Jinpa, Jana Haritatos, and Steve Cole for your inspiration, support on interpreting research, and incredible generosity in sharing your wisdom.

To the Compassion Institute and all the amazing people I am lucky to have as friends and colleagues, especially KC Branscomb, Kirk Hanson, Margaret Cullen, Erika Rosenberg, and Monica Hanson.

To the Center for Compassion and Altruism, Research, and Education (CCARE), specifically Dr. Jim Doty, Monica Worline, and Emma Seppala, who have done so much to support compassion in the world of research and beyond.

And this acknowledgment list would not be complete without a giant nod to the Stanford Graduate School of Business. Thank you for accepting me, taking me into your fold, and allowing me to connect with such brilliant people as Jon Levin, Sarah Soule, Yossi Feinberg, Sarah Stone, and Leslie Chin, among many, many, others.

Lastly, to my students: you have taught me more than you know through your formidable intelligence, heart, soul, and candor.

With Thanks and Gratitude.

Notes

Introduction

1. Kate Davidson, "Employers Find 'Soft Skills' Like Critical Thinking in Short Supply," *Wall Street Journal*, Aug. 30, 2016.

2. Guy Berger, "Soft Skills Are Increasingly Crucial to Getting Your Dream Job," LinkedIn, 2016, https://www.linkedin.com/pulse/soft-skills-increasingly-crucial-getting-your-dream-guy-berger-ph-d-.

Chapter 1: Healing the Toxic Workplace

1. Pawel Wargocki, David P. Wyon, Yong K. Baik, Geo Clausen, and P. Ole Fanger, "Perceived Air Quality, Sick Building Syndrome (SBS) Symptoms and Productivity in an Office with Two Different Pollution Loads," *Indoor Air* 9, no. 3 (1999): 165–79.

2. Ahmed Mazroei, Amit Kaushik, and Esam Elsarrag, "Impact of Indoor Environmental Quality on Occupant Well-Being and Comfort: A Review of the Literature," *International Journal of Sustainable Built Environment* 5, no. 1 (2016): 1–11, doi:10.1016/j.ijsbe.2016.03.006.

3. Joseph G. Allen, Piers MacNaughton, Usha Satish, Suresh Santanam, Jose Vallarino, and John D. Spengler, "Associations of Cognitive Function Scores with Carbon Dioxide, Ventilation, and Volatile Organic Compound Exposures in Office Workers: A Controlled Exposure Study of Green and Conventional Office Environments," *Environmental Health Perspectives* (online) 124, no. 6 (2016): 805, doi:10.1289/ehp.1510037.

4. Wendy Stubbs and Chris Cocklin, "An Ecological Modernist Interpretation of Sustainability: The Case of Interface Inc.," *Business Strategy and the Environment* 17, no. 8 (2008): 512.

5. Ray Anderson, "The Business Logic of Sustainability, TED Talk, Feb. 2009, https://www.ted.com/talks/ray_anderson_on_the_business_logic_of_sustainability/transcript?language=en.

6. Paul Hawken, *The Ecology of Commerce: A Declaration of Sustainability* (New York: Collins Business, 1993).

7. National Public Radio, Robert Wood Johnson Foundation, and Harvard T. H. Chan School of Public Health, "The Workplace and Health," May 2016, http://www .npr.org/documents/2016/jul/Workplace-Health-Poll.pdf.

8. Rebecca Ray, Milla Sanes, and John Schmitt, "No-Vacation Nation Revisited," Center for Economic and Policy Research, May 2003, http://cepr.net/documents /publications/no-vacation-update-2013-05.pdf.

9. Mika Kivimäki, Markus Jokela, Solja T. Nyberg, Archana Singh-Manoux, Eleonor I. Fransson, Lars Alfredsson, Jakob B. Bjorner et al., "Long Working Hours and Risk of Coronary Heart Disease and Stroke: A Systematic Review and Meta-Analysis of Published and Unpublished Data for 603,838 Individuals." *The Lancet* 386, no. 10005 (2015): 1739–46.

10. American Psychological Association, "Stress in America Survey," American Psychological Association, 2007, http://www.apa.org/news/press/releases/stress/index .aspx.

11. Peter J. Frost, "Why Compassion Counts!" *Journal of Management Inquiry* 20, no. 4 (1999): 395–401.

12. Jeffrey Pfeffer, "Why the Assholes Are Winning: Money Trumps All," *Journal of Management Studies* 53, no. 4 (2016).

13. Ibid.

14. Rakesh Khurana and Nitin Nohria, "It's Time to Make Management a True Profession," *Harvard Business Review* 86, no. 10 (2008): 70–77.

15. Robert S. Rubin and Erich C. Dierdorff, "How Relevant Is the MBA? Assessing the Alignment of Required Curricula and Required Managerial Competencies," *Academy of Management Learning and Education* 8, no. 2 (2009): 208–24.

16. Mark Murphy, *Hiring for Attitude* (New York: McGraw-Hill, 2012).

17. "What's Your Major? 4 Decades of College Degrees, in 1 Graph," *Planet Money*, May 9, 2014, http://www.npr.org/sections/money/2014/05/09/310114739/whats-your -major-four-decades-of-college-degrees-in-1-graph.

18. Yoni Appelbaum, "Why America's Business Majors Are in Desperate Need of a Liberal-Arts Education," *The Atlantic*, June 28, 2016, https://www.theatlantic.com /business/archive/2016/06/why-americas-business-majors-are-in-desperate-need -of-a-liberal-arts-education/489209/.

19. Davidson, "Employers Find 'Soft Skills' Like Critical Thinking in Short Supply."

20. Guy Berger, "Soft Skills Are Increasingly Crucial to Getting Your Dream Job," LinkedIn, 2016, https://www.linkedin.com/pulse/soft-skills-increasingly-crucial -getting-your-dream-guy-berger-ph-d-.

21. Dan Schawbel, "Arianna Huffington: Why Entrepreneurs Should Embrace the Third Metric," *Forbes*, March 25, 2014.

Chapter 2: Full-Catastrophe Working

1. Jon Kabat-Zinn, *Full Catastrophe Living: Using the Wisdom of Your Body and Mind to Face Stress, Pain, and Illness: The Mindfulness-Based Stress Reduction (MBSR) Program Used in Medical Centers Worldwide* (New York: Bantam Books, 2013), 1.

2. Elizabeth H. Blackburn, "Telomeres and Telomerase: The Means to the End (Nobel lecture)," *Angewandte Chemie International Edition* 49, no. 41 (2010): 7405–21.

3. Elissa S. Epel, Elizabeth H. Blackburn, Jue Lin, Firdaus S. Dhabhar, Nancy E. Adler, Jason D. Morrow, and Richard M. Cawthon, "Accelerated Telomere Shortening in Response to Life Stress," *Proceedings of the National Academy of Sciences of the United States of America* 101, no. 49 (2004): 17312–15.

4. Ibid.

5. "The Rat Dog," episode of *Curb Your Enthusiasm*.

6. John Lahr, "Petrified: The Horrors of Stagefright," *The New Yorker*, Aug. 28, 2006, 38–42.

7. Anita Singh, "Addicts Symphony: Drink and Drugs 'Widespread in Classical World,' Says Cellist," *The Telegraph*, Aug. 19, 2014, http://www.telegraph.co.uk/culture/tvandradio/11041804/Addicts-Symphony-drink-and-drugs-widespread-in-classical-world-says-cellist.html.

8. Anselm Doll, Britta K. Hölzel, Satja Mulej Bratec, Christine C. Boucard, Xiyao Xie, Afra M. Wohlschläger, Christian Sorg, "Mindful Attention to Breath Regulates Emotions via Increased Amygdala–Prefrontal Cortex Connectivity," *NeuroImage* 134 (July 1, 2016), 305–13; https://doi.org/10.1016/j.neuroimage.2016.03.041.

9. Elke Vlemincx, Ilse Van Diest, Omer Van den Bergh, "A Sigh of Relief or a Sigh to Relieve: The Psychological and Physiological Relief Effect of Deep Breaths," *Physiology and Behavior* 165 (October 15, 2016), 127–35; https://doi.org/10.1016/j.physbeh.2016.07.004.

10. https://www.researchgate.net/publication/263746643_The_Brain-Gut_Axis_in_Health_and_Disease.

11. http://ei.yale.edu/story/student-age-6-elementary-school/.

12. Ibid.

13. Ronald Abadian Heifetz, Alexander Grashow, and Martin Linsky, *The Practice of Adaptive Leadership: Tools and Tactics for Changing Your Organization and the World* (Boston: Harvard Business Press, 2009).

14. Mahzarin R. Banaji, Max H. Bazerman, Dolly Chugh, "How Unethical Are You?" *Harvard Business Review*, Dec. 2003. https://hbr.org/2003/12/how-unethical-are-you?

15. Amy Wrzesniewski and Jane E. Dutton, "Crafting a Job: Revisioning Employees as Active Crafters of Their Work," *Academy of Management Review* 26, no. 2 (2001): 179–201.

Chapter 3: On Purpose (with a Capital *P*)

1. Amy Wrzesniewski and Jane E. Dutton, "Crafting a Job: Revisioning Employees as Active Crafters of Their Work," *Academy of Management Review* 26, no. 2 (2001): 179–201.

2. Barbara L. Fredrickson, Karen M. Grewen, Kimberly A. Coffey, Sara B. Algoe, Ann M. Firestine, Jesusa M. G. Arevalo, Jeffrey Ma, and Steven W. Cole, "A Functional Genomic Perspective on Human Well-Being," *Proceedings of the National Academy of Sciences* 110, no. 33 (2013): 13684–89.

3. Ibid.

4. Samuel Cohen, Chirag Bavishi, Alan Rozanski, "Purpose in Life and Its Relationship to All-Cause Mortality and Cardiovascular Events," *Psychosomatic Medicine* 78, no. 2 (Feb.–Mar. 2016): 1, doi:10.1097/PSY.0000000000000274.

5. Alia J. Crum and Ellen J. Langer, "Mind-Set Matters Exercise and the Placebo Effect," *Psychological Science* 18, no. 2 (2007): 165–71.

6. Anthony L. Burrow, Maclen Stanley, Rachel Sumner, and Patrick L. Hill. "Purpose in Life as a Resource for Increasing Comfort with Ethnic Diversity," *Personality and Social Psychology Bulletin* 40, no. 11 (2014): 1507–16.

7. Anthony L. Burrow and Patrick L. Hill, "Derailed by Diversity? Purpose Buffers the Relationship Between Ethnic Composition on Trains and Passenger Negative Mood," *Personality and Social Psychology Bulletin* 39, no. 12 (2013), doi:10.1177/0146167213499377.

8. Abraham Harold Maslow, "A Theory of Human Motivation," *Psychological Review* 50, no. 4 (1943): 370.

9. Kendall Cotton Bronk, "Kendall Cotton Bronk on Talking to Youth about Purpose," YouTube, April 4, 2017, https://www.youtube.com/watch?v=bo80mPL4DDs.

10. Pema Chödrön, *Start Where You Are: A Guide to Compassionate Living* (Boston: Shambhala, 2004).

11. Mihaly Csikszentmihalyi, *Flow: The Psychology of Optimal Experience* (New York: Harper Perennial Modern Classics, 2009).

Chapter 4: Cultivating Compassion

1. Christine L. Porath and Christine M. Pearson, "The Cost of Bad Behavior," *Organizational Dynamics* 39, no. 1 (2010): 64–71.

2. Christine L. Porath, Trevor Foulk, and Amir Erez, "How Incivility Hijacks Performance: It Robs Cognitive Resources, Increases Dysfunctional Behavior, and Infects Team Dynamics and Functioning," *Organizational Dynamics* (Jan. 2015), https://www.researchgate.net/profile/Christine_Porath/publication/285770782
_How_Incivility_Hijacks_Performance_It_Robs_Cognitive_Resources_Increases
_Dysfunctional_Behavior_and_Infects_Team_Dynamics_and_Functioning/links
/56635f4308ae4931cd5edc20/.

3. Career Builder, "One-in-Four Workers Have Felt Bullied in the Workplace, CareerBuilder Study Finds-CareerBuilder," April 20, 2011, http://www.careerbuilder.com/share/aboutus/pressreleasesdetail.aspx?id=pr632&sd=4%2F20%2F2011&ed=4%2F20%2F2099.

4. American Psychological Association, "Don't Let Workplace Stress Ruin Your Labor Day Holiday," APA.org, http://www.apa.org/helpcenter/labor-day.aspx.

5. J. S. House, K. R. Landis, and D. Umberson, "Social Relationships and Health," *Science,* American Association for the Advancement of Science, July 29, 1988.

6. Charles Darwin, *The Descent of Man* (New York: American Home Library, 1902), 72.

7. Brian G. Knutson, Elliott Wimmer, Camelia M. Kuhnen, and Piotr Winkielman, "Nucleus Accumbens Activation Mediates the Influence of Reward Cues on Financial Risk Taking," *NeuroReport* 19, no. 5 (2008): 509–13.

8. LinkedIn Compassion (https://www.linkedin.com/pulse/20121015034012-22330283-managing-compassionately/).

9. "Women in the Workplace 2016," McKinsey and Company Organization, http://www.mckinsey.com/business-functions/organization/our-insights/women-in-the-workplace-2016.

10. Ibid.

11. John M. Darley and C. Daniel Batson, "From Jerusalem to Jericho": A Study of Situational and Dispositional Variables in Helping Behavior," *Journal of Personality and Social Psychology* 27, no. 1 (1973): 100.

12. Tracy L. Spinrad and Cynthia A. Stifter, "Toddlers' Empathy-Related Responding to Distress: Predictions from Negative Emotionality and Maternal Behavior in Infancy," *Infancy* 10, no. 2 (2006): 97–121, http://hhd.psu.edu/ebp/documents/spinradstifter2006.pdf.

Chapter 5: Dealing with Ourselves

1. J. R. Joeng and S. L. Turner, "Mediators Between Self-Criticism and Depression: Fear of Compassion, Self-Compassion, and Importance to Others," *Journal of Counseling Psychology,* advance online publication, http://self-compassion.org/wp-content/uploads/2015/08/Joeng_SC_Fear-of-SC.pdf.

2. Claire E. Adams and Mark R. Leary, "Promoting Self-Compassionate Attitudes Toward Eating Among Restrictive and Guilty Eaters," *Journal of Social and Clinical Psychology* 26, no. 10 (2007): 1120–44.

3. Kristin Neff, "Self-Compassion: An Alternative Conceptualization of a Healthy Attitude Toward Oneself," *Self and Identity* 2, no. 2 (2003): 85–101.

4. https://www.wsj.com/articles/the-key-to-getting-workers-to-stop-wasting-time-online-1457921545

5. Ying Wong and Jeanne Tsai, "Cultural Models of Shame and Guilt," in *The Self-Conscious Emotions: Theory and Research*, ed. Jessica L. Tracy, Richard W. Robins, and June Price Tangney (New York: Guilford Press, 2007): 209–23.

6. CDC Foundation, "Worker Illness and Injury Costs [sic] U.S. Employers $225.8 Billion Annually," CDCFoundation.org, Jan. 28, 2015, https://www.cdcfoundation .org/pr/2015/worker-illness-and-injury-costs-us-employers-225-billion-annually.

7. Jean M. Twenge and Joshua D. Foster, "Birth Cohort Increases in Narcissistic Personality Traits Among American College Students, 1982–2009," *Social Psychological and Personality Science* 1, no. 1 (2010): 99–106.

Chapter 6: The Wisdom of Emotions

1. Viktor E. Frankl, *Man's Search for Meaning* (New York: Simon & Schuster, 1997).

2. Susan Candiotti, "Cursing, Beer and a Popped Chute as Flight Attendant Quits," CNN, Aug. 10, 2010, http://www.cnn.com/2010/TRAVEL/08/09/new.york.escape.chute.opened/.

3. James J. Gross and Oliver P. John, "Individual Differences in Two Emotion Regulation Processes: Implications for Affect, Relationships, and Well-Being," *Journal of Personality and Social Psychology* 85, no. 2 (2003): 348.

4. Anne Kreamer, *It's Always Personal: Emotion in the New Workplace* (New York: Random House, 2011).

5. Antoine Gara, "Billionaire Bill Gross Settles 'Cabal' Lawsuit with Bond Giant Pimco After 2014 Ouster," Forbes, March 27, 2017, https://www.forbes.com/sites /antoinegara/2017/03/27/billionaire-bill-gross-settles-cabal-lawsuit-with-bond-giant -pimco-after-2014-ouster/#2bbb31f71015.

6. David F. Larcker and Brian Tayan, "Scoundrels in the C-Suite: How Should the Board Respond When a CEO's Bad Behavior Makes the News?" Stanford Closer Look Series, May 10, 2016, https://www.gsb.stanford.edu/sites/gsb/files/publication -pdf/cgri-closer-look-57-scoundrels-csuite.pdf.

7. Daniel Kahneman, *Thinking, Fast and Slow* (New York: Macmillan, 2011).

8. Jonathan Haidt, "The Emotional Dog and Its Rational Tail: A Social Intuitionist Approach to Moral Judgment," *Psychological Review* 108, no. 4 (2001): 814.

9. Benjamin P. Chapman, Kevin Fiscella, Ichiro Kawachi, Paul Duberstein, and Peter Muennig, "Emotion Suppression and Mortality Risk over a 12-year Follow-up," *Journal of Psychosomatic Research* 75, no. 4 (2013): 381–85.

10. Susannah Fox and Maeve Duggan, "Tracking for Health," Pew Research Center: Internet, Science & Tech, Jan. 27, 2013, http://www.pewinternet.org/2013/01/28 /tracking-for-health/.

11. David Foster Wallace, Commencement address (delivered at Kenyon College, Gambier, OH, May 21, 2005), https://web.ics.purdue.edu/~drkelly/DFWKenyon Address2005.pdf.

12. Sheldon Cohen, "Social Relationships and Health," *American Psychologist* 59, no. 8 (November 2004), 676–84.

Chapter 7: Fail Better

1. Todd Bishop, "Bill Gates and Paul Allen Had a Business Before Microsoft, and This Engineer Was Their Partner," GeekWire, March 27, 2017, https://www.geekwire.com/2017/bill-gates-paul-allen-business-microsoft-engineer-partner/.

2. Giada Di Stefano, Francesca Gino, Gary P. Pisano, and Bradley R. Staats, "Making Experience Count: The Role of Reflection in Individual Learning," Harvard Business School Working Paper 14–093, 2016, http://www.hbs.edu/faculty/Publication%20Files/14–093_defe8327-eeb6–40c3-aafe-26194181cfd2.pdf.

3. C. Copley and B. Hirschler, "For Roche CEO, Celebrating Failure Is Key to Success," Reuters, Sept. 17, 2014, http://www.reuters.com/article/roche-ceo-failure-idUSL6N0RI18H20140917.

4. Ibid.

5. Carol S. Dweck, *Mindset: The New Psychology of Success* (New York: Random House, 2008).

6. Susan J. Ashford and D. Scott DeRue, "Developing as a Leader: The Power of Mindful Engagement," *Organizational Dynamics* 41, no. 2 (2012): 146–54.

7. Umair Haque, "The Generation M Manifesto," *Harvard Business Review,* June 15, 2015, https://hbr.org/2009/07/today-in-capitalism-20–1.

8. Fredrickson, Grewen, Coffey, Algoe, Firestine, Arevalo, Ma, and Cole, "A Functional Genomic Perspective on Human Well-Being," 13684–89.

9. Yasuhiro Yamakawa, Mike W. Peng, and David L. Deeds, "What Drives New Ventures to Internationalize from Emerging to Developed Economies?" *Entrepreneurship Theory and Practice* 32, no. 1 (2008): 59–82.

10. http://ir.library.louisville.edu/etd/2304/?utm_source=ir.library.louisville.edu%2Fetd%2F2304&utm_medium=PDF&utm_campaign=PDFCoverPages.

11. https://link.com/article/10.1007/s10862–015–9510–1.

12. Ibid.

13. http://www.pnas.org/content/112/28/8567.short.

14. Andrew P. Hill and Thomas Curran, "Multidimensional Perfectionism and Burnout: A Meta-Analysis," *Personality and Social Psychology Review* 20, no. 3 (2016): 269–88.

15. Jack Zenger and Joseph Folkman, "Your Employees Want the Negative Feedback You Hate to Give," *Harvard Business Review,* April 11, 2017.

16. Ibid.

17. Ibid.

242   Notes

18. John Mordechai Gottman, *What Predicts Divorce? The Relationship Between Marital Processes and Marital Outcomes* (Hillsdale, NJ: Lawrence Erlbaum Associates, 1994).

19. Kelly Lambert, Molly Hyer, Massimo Bardi, Amanda Rzucidlo, Samantha Scott, Brennan Terhune-Cotter, Ashley Hazelgrove, Ilton Silva, and Craig Kinsley, "Natural-Enriched Environments Lead to Enhanced Environmental Engagement and Altered Neurobiological Resilience," *Neuroscience* 330 (2016): 386–94.

Chapter 8: How Courage Makes Us More Resilient

1. Howard Berkes, "30 Years After Explosion, Challenger Engineer Still Blames Himself," NPR.org, Jan. 28, 2016, http://www.npr.org/sections/thetwo-way/2016/01/28/464744781/30-years-after-disaster-challenger-engineer-still-blames-himself.

2. Christopher Peterson and Martin E. P. Seligman, *Character Strengths and Virtues: A Handbook and Classification* (Oxford: Oxford University Press, 2004).

3. Abby Goodnough, Monica Davey, and Mitch Smith, "When the Water Turned Brown," *New York Times,* Jan. 23, 2016, https://www.nytimes.com/2016/01/24/us/when-the-water-turned-brown.html?_r=0.

4. Christopher J. Keller, "Courage, Psychological Well-Being, and Somatic Symptoms," PhD dissertation, Seattle Pacific University, 2016, http://digitalcommons.spu.edu/cgi/viewcontent.cgi?article=1016&context=cpy_etd.

5. Ibid.

6. Ibid.

7. Phillip Zimbardo, "What Makes a Hero?," *Greater Good Magazine,* Jan. 18, 2011, http://greatergood.berkeley.edu/article/item/what_makes_a_hero.

8. "34% of Employees Do Not Speak Up Because of Fear of Retribution," *Decision-Wise,* July 15, 2015, https://www.decision-wise.com/decisionwise-benchmark-study/.

9. Nemeth, Charlan Jeanne, and Joel Wachtler, "Creative problem solving as a result of majority vs minority influence." *European Journal of Social Psychology* 13, no. 1 (1983): 45–55.

10. http://www.businessnewsdaily.com/9612-silent-employees-cost-companies.html.

11. Pauline Schilpzand, David R. Hekman, and Terence R. Mitchell, "An Inductively Generated Typology and Process Model of Workplace Courage," *Organization Science* 26, no. 1 (2014): 52–77.

12. Ethan R. Burris, "The Risks and Rewards of Speaking Up: Managerial Responses to Employee Voice," *Academy of Management Journal* 55, no. 4 (2012): 851–75.

13. Jennifer J. Kish-Gephart, James R. Detert, Linda Klebe Treviño, and Amy C. Edmondson, "Silenced by Fear: The Nature, Sources, and Consequences of Fear at Work," *Research in Organizational Behavior* 29 (2009): 163–93.

14. Kathleen K. Reardon, "Courage as a Skill," *Harvard Business Review*, July 31, 2014, https://hbr.org/2007/01/courage-as-a-skill.

15. Michelle Harbour and Veronika Kisfalvi, "In the Eye of the Beholder: An Exploration of Managerial Courage," *Journal of Business Ethics* 119, no. 4 (2014): 493–515.

Chapter 9: Purposeful Organizations

1. Jeffrey Pfeffer, "Why Deception Is Probably the Single Most Important Leadership Skill," Fortune, June 2, 2016, http://fortune.com/2016/06/02/lying-leadership-skills-expectations-communication.

Index

Index

About the Author

Leah Weiss, PhD, is a researcher, professor, consultant, and author. She teaches courses on compassionate leadership at the Stanford Graduate School of Business and is the principal teacher and founding faculty for Stanford's Compassion Cultivation Program, conceived by the Dalai Lama. She also directs compassion education and scholarship at HopeLab, an Omidyar Group research-and-development nonprofit focused on resilience. She lives in Palo Alto, California, with her husband and three children.